MW01232894

A
WORKSHOP
ON

Self-Giving

Books in the Workshop Series

A
WORKSHOP
ON

Self-Giving

MARILYN N. ANDERES

Lamplighter
Books Grand Rapids,
Michigan
Zondervan Publishing House

Special Thanks to
My Spiritual Parents, George and Carol Anderson,
and the Family at
Mount Oak United Methodist Church,
Mitchellville, Maryland
For Their Encouragement and Life,
and to
Marilyn Sue and Paul Bowser
For Their Expertise in Editing and Typing

A Workshop on Self-Giving
Copyright © 1989 by Marilyn N. Anderes

Lamplighter Books are published by the Zondervan Publishing House
1415 Lake Drive, S.E., Grand Rapids, Michigan 49506

ISBN 0-310-52251-X

Edited by Martha Manikas-Foster, John Sloan

Printed in the United States of America

89 90 91 92 93 / PP / 10 9 8 7 6 5 4 3 2 1

*This work is dedicated
to my husband, John,
who daily lives
the message
of this book.*

CONTENTS

FOREWORD

A great conductor was once asked: "What is the most difficult instrument to play in the full orchestra?" He responded: "It is, without a doubt, second fiddle."

It's true. Being second, or even last, is difficult for any of us. Yet, sometimes that's what God asks of his mature followers.

The One who emptied himself for us, giving all that he had, knows that great joy is ours when we learn to give. What is this giving he exemplifies? It is generous, whole-hearted, and free—free, but not cheap. When we give ourselves to him and we grow up in the faith, even a little bit, we desire to follow his example. The cost is ourselves. The priority is no longer good *self*-image but rather that we might mirror *his* image, learning to lay down our lives for others.

Come along. Let's learn together how to be virtuosos at "second fiddle."

BOOK OVERVIEW

Chap.	Title	Subject	Scripture Text	Key Verse(s)	Example
1	"Me? Wash Feet?"	The Essence of Giving	John 13:1–17	Mark 10:45	Jesus
2	A Prepared Heart	Shaping Attitudes	Rom. 7 & 8	Ps. 27:8	Paul
3	One-Way Traffic. Yield!	Being a Yielder	Matt. 1:18–25	Eph. 5:21	Mary's Joseph
4	Forgery or Original Masterpiece?	Being Vulnerable	Neh. 1 & 2	2 Cor. 3:16	Nehemiah
5	Earning the Title: Diplomat	Being a Reconciler	2 Cor. 5	Rom. 12:18	Zacchaeus and Joseph
6	Defender or Prosecutor?	Being a Wise Reprover	2 Sam. 12:1–15	Col. 1:28	Nathan
7	The Tug-of-War	Being Committed to a Good Report	Luke 1:5–45	Prov. 18:21	Elizabeth
8	Helping Hands	Being a Life-Sharer	1 Sam. 18–20	Gal. 6:2	Jonathan
9	Choosing Second Place	Being a Builder of Success in Others	Judges 4	Phil. 2:3–4	Deborah
10	Looking in the Keyhole	Being Cheerfully Hospitable	2 Kings 4:8–17	1 Peter 4:9	Shunammite Woman
11	Keyboard Harmony	Being a Lover of the Unlovely	Acts 9	Matt. 5:46–48	Ananias
12	Whistle While You Work	Being an Excellent Example in the Mundane	Ruth 2	Luke 16:10	Ruth

GUIDELINES FOR GROUP LEADERS

Several options are open for any Bible study group. As the leader, you should know your group's needs best and be able to tailor the material to the people. Here are three considerations.

Options	Individual Work	Group Work	Leader's Work	This Option's Benefits
OPTION ONE	Do memory verse and preparation references before group meeting. Application questions after group meeting.	Do all the Discovery questions together. Pray!	Pray before, during, and after group meeting; assign verses for Discovery questions; keep discussion on target; watch time allotment.	Best for a larger group that doesn't know each other well or one that would not be comfortable sharing personal life applications.
OPTION TWO	Do memory verse and preparation references and specific Discovery questions (not all of them).	Report on specific Discovery questions assigned. Share applications and insights. Pray!	Pray! Assign Discovery questions at previous meeting. Monitor discussion and time.	Most any group could use this option. Not good for groups unwilling to be vulnerable.
OPTION THREE	Do memory verse, preparation references, Discovery questions, and application. Pray!	Share insight gained from private study. Do application together. Encourage each other. Pray!	Pray! Keep sharing on target. Choose major topics to discuss. Monitor time.	Best for a smaller, more mature group; one disciplined to do the work alone, to be vulnerable, and to keep confidences.

1

"ME? WASH FEET?"
The Essence of Giving

Memory Verse: Mark 10:45

"You're not gonna like this Mom. The dog's knocked over another plant." Sunlight streamed into my neighbor's living room window, spotlighting the collage of dirt, pebbles, clay pot pieces, peat moss . . . and dog hair. The pungent odor of fertilizer cut the air. It was the fourth accident this week. "I should've sent our dog to the kennel last week when we were on vacation, then I wouldn't have to watch after the neighbor's dog to pay them back. Stupid dog! I didn't bargain for this. I only agreed to feed the animal. I've done all I was asked to do for the dog, and at exactly the right times."

Muddy water spilled as I slapped the brush down. Careful to leave the cleaning tools in an obvious place, I slammed the door behind me. My neighbors would surely notice that I had had to do extra duty. "Stupid dog!"

It's hard to stoop down and live sacrificially, but mature believers are asked to give of themselves. Most of us don't refuse giving, but we often give selfishly—only to those who applaud us, or to those we know will repay us, or to those we're responsible for. We give what is expected, but not much more. It's our old nature to be takers, but we don't have to settle for that. We can work toward the potential God sees for us. We can grow up—learn how to be givers, not just getters—and allow selfishness to be replaced by joy in sacrifice.

In this lesson we will discover that the essence of giving is sacrificial living. And, with love as our motive, we will learn that laying down our lives for others *defines* sacrificial living.

DISCOVERY 1: THE ESSENCE OF GIVING

Webster's definition of the verb "give" is: "To bestow without a return."[1]

1. What did God give in John 3:16? _____

2. What did he give himself for according to 1 Tim. 2:5–6? _____

_____

3. Read Isa. 53:12; Phil. 2:7; Rom. 8:32; and Eph. 1:7–8. What adjectives describe God's giving? _____

_____

4. a. According to John 3:16, *what* did God give? _____

b. How many sons did he have to give? _____

c. Reread the first part of the verse. *Why* did he give us so much? _____

_____

[1] *Webster's New Collegiate Dictionary* (Springfield, Massachusetts: G. & C. Merriam Co., Publishers, 1961), 350.

d. What was Jesus' command to us in John 15:12? _____

_____

e. According to John 15:13 *how* does he love? _____

_____

f. How should *we* love? (See 1 John 3:16.) _____

_____

5. a. Read what Jesus had to say in Mark 10:42–45. What must we do to become great (v. 43)? _____

b. To be first of all, what must we do (v. 44)? _____

_____

c. What example did he provide in v. 45? _____

_____

DISCOVERY 2: WHY I SHOULD WANT TO GIVE BEYOND WHAT'S EXPECTED

1. a. According to Luke 6:38, is giving a suggestion or a command? _____

_____

b. According to John 15:12–13, is laying down your life a suggestion or a command? _____

c. What is the right response to a command that God gives (John 14:15)? _____

d. Should it be burdensome (1 John 5:2–3)? _____

e. Why not? _____

_____

f. According to John 14:21, what happens when we obey God's commands? _____

2. a. According to Eph. 2:8–9 and Titus 3:5–7, what are we saved by? _____

b. According to Eph. 2:10 and Titus 3:8, what are we saved for? _____

c. Why? (Read Matt. 5:16 and 1 Peter 2:12.) _____

_____

3. Read Phil. 2:3–8 and decide what example we should follow and with what attitude? _____

_____

4. According to Matt. 16:23, whose interests should we be seeking? _____

_____

5. Read Heb. 13:20–21. Why should we live sacrificially?

_____

_____

6. What does Matt. 5:41–48 challenge us to do? _____

_____

_____

7. The people for whom we lay down our lives are important. What would a mature attitude be toward them? Read Rom. 15:1–3. _____

_____

_____

8. Read 2 Tim. 2:10. If we have a sacrificial attitude, whom should we *desire* to introduce others to? _____

9. According to 2 Cor. 5:14–15, what should control us, enabling us to live a sacrificial life? _____

_____

10. Although we do not give in order to get, does God give us anything in return (see Luke 6:38)? _____

_____

_____

_____

DISCOVERY 3: TO LAY DOWN MY LIFE AND GIVE SACRIFICIALLY

Christ's example of giving by laying down his life is, of course, most dramatic at Calvary. But he lived sacrificially before Golgotha. When Jesus laid down his life, he was really doing three things:

1. He was abiding in the Father's love.
2. He was being separate unto God.
3. He was being a second-miler.

Some of us have been Christians for a long time. Yet, we have not been willing to accept God's love and put Christ first in everything. We are often not set apart for his special use. Nor do we go out of our way for anyone. We need to follow Jesus' example when he washed the disciples' feet.

Read John 13:1–17 and transport yourself to the Upper Room. Pretend to be a disciple with your senses alive and keen.

The King of Kings has risen from the table, tying an ordinary towel around his waist. The things he brought to dinner with him have been tossed aside so he can be free to refresh you. He goes for a basin and pours water into it, stooping down to wash dust from your crusty feet. He gives no thought about getting dirt on himself. Answer the following questions with a disciple's sensitivity. (Perhaps closing your eyes would help your imagination.)

1. What does the room look like? _____

_____

_____

2. What tastes are still in your mouth from dinner? _____

_____

3. What mundane tools is Jesus using to give you the gift of refreshment? _____

4. What smells are you aware of? _____

_____

5. What sounds do you hear in the room? _____

_____

6. How does it feel to have your feet washed? _____

_____

7. What are you thinking as the Master washes your feet?

_____

_____

_____

_____

Answer the following questions to see what Jesus was really doing when he washed the feet of his friends.

Jesus was abiding in the Father's love

1. What three things did Jesus know for sure in John 13:3?

    a. _____

b. _____

c. _____

2. a. How did this security help Jesus live sacrificially? (Read Phil. 2:5–8 to help you answer the question.)

_____

_____

  b. What does 2 Peter 1:3 say God has given us? _____

_____

  c. What does Jer. 31:3 say? _____

_____

  d. How does John 1:12 describe us? _____

_____

  e. Read John 14:2–3. What has God prepared for us?

_____

_____

  f. According to Phil. 2:3–5, what can we do now? _____

_____

What are we really doing when we lay down our lives? We are abiding in the Father's love.

Jesus was separate unto God

  1. What did Jesus do in John 13:4–5 that made him different from the others at the table? _____

_____

  2. a. What question did Jesus ask in John 13:12? _____

_____

b. How were his actions significant? _____

_____

c. Is it hard for you to want to get up to do the dishes after eating with delightful company? _____

d. What motivates you to get up and get moving? _____

_____

3. Jesus was set apart for God's special use. We are capable of laying down our lives for others when we choose to set ourselves apart for God's use. What does Deut. 7:6 say? _____

What are we really doing when we lay down our lives? We are choosing to set ourselves apart for God's special use. We don't have to be like everyone else.

Jesus was being a second-miler

1. a. Who was Jesus recognized to be in John 13:13? _____

_____

b. Who was the honored guest? _____

c. What special acclaim had been given to Jesus earlier in the week (John 12:12–13)? _____

d. According to John 12–16, had the disciples listened intently or casually to Jesus' words that week? _____

2. Who ordinarily washed guests' feet? (See a Bible dictionary to find the answer.) _____

3. According to John 13:14–16, what example did Jesus want the disciples—and us—to follow? _____

4. What do you think was the motivation for Jesus' actions (John 13:11, 34–35)? _____

_____

5. Read Matt. 5:40–41. What does v. 41 tell us to do?

_____

_____

What are we really doing when we lay down our lives? We are going the second mile.

DISCOVERY 4: APPLICATION

Maturity comes as we turn everything over to Jesus Christ. A grown-up disciple yields thoughts, words, intentions, actions, and relationships to him. This can't help but turn the old nature of selfishness into the new nature of sacrifice with rejoicing. A mature follower of Christ can and does get the basin, pour the water, get the towel ready, and wash dusty, smelly feet.

Take a long hard look at your life. Can you honestly say that you have made choices that take you beyond the convenient and comfortable ways of life? Have you allowed God to use you in *his* caring of the world? Have you given as he gives, laying down your life for others?

After you have finished with the following illustration, rate yourself on the maturity chart that follows it. Read each statement carefully and record your responses by making a check in the column that describes you best.

Identify your present attitude about sacrificial living. Pray. Ask God to touch your heart with his thoughts about sacrificing yourself for others. Consider the questions on the illustration on the next page, and write specific responses. Ask God to give you the names of people for whom you can lay down your life.

How Are You
Abiding in
God's Love?

How Are You Set
Apart for Him?

How Are You Going the Second
Mile in Anyone's Life?

Whose Feet Will You Wash?

Mature Christian Giving	Always	Almost Always	Frequently	Sometimes	Never
1. I give myself to God by being rightly related to him through Jesus Christ.					
2. I give myself to God by being available to him so that he can work through me.					
3. I give myself to God by being able to stand alone.					

Mature Christian Giving	Always	Almost Always	Frequently	Sometimes	Never
4. I give myself to God by being still before him consistently.					
5. I give myself to God by seeing his interests in others.					
6. I give myself to God by being diligent, eager to work for him, but careful.					
7. I give myself to God by choosing faith, not feelings, to rule my life.					
8. I give myself to God by being content with reality, not fantasy. I know God is in control and he loves me, a sinner.					
9. I give myself to God by considering his Word to be my very life.					
10. I give myself to God by trusting in him, not my own understanding.					
11. I give myself to God and others by sacrificially giving time, money, and energy.					
12. I give myself to God and others by drawing my security from a right relationship with the Father.					

Mature Christian Giving	Always	Almost Always	Frequently	Sometimes	Never
13. I give myself to God and others by having my priorities in order: 1. God 2. Spouse 3. Children 4. Ministry.					
14. I give myself to God and others by being vulnerable (open and honest) with them.					
15. I give myself to God and others by using discernment for intercession and, if God leads, loving reproof.					
16. I give myself to God and others by being teachable—able to receive reproof.					
17. I give myself to God and others by loving the unlovely.					
18. I give myself to God and others by being excited to excel in the mundane.					
19. I give myself to God and others by being a bold but gentle witness for him.					
20. I give myself to God and others by deferring first, to God, and then, to others.					

Mature Christian Giving	Always	Almost Always	Frequently	Sometimes	Never
21. I give myself to God and others by being willing to be the first to reconcile broken relationships.					
22. I give myself to God and others by being committed to giving good reports.					
23. I give myself to God and others by being willing to share in fellowship with responsibility and accountability.					
24. I give myself to God and others by practicing cheerful hospitality.					
25. I give myself to God and others by working to make them successful in God's plan.					

You should now be aware of some of your strengths and weaknesses. If you have just come to know Jesus, don't be too hard on yourself. You need time to grow. If you gave your life to Christ some time ago and the chart reveals more weaknesses than strengths, then ask God for help and purpose to grow up.

You might even be that rare individual who gives *too* much; you see lots of needs and feel that *you* are the one to meet them all. That's out of balance, too. Go back to giving yourself to God alone for awhile and let him direct your steps with others. Wherever you are on the chart, strive to measure up to God's plan for you right now in your giving. Lay down your life for others.

A Parting Thought

> *"Don't conduct your life*
> *on the cafeteria plan—self-service only."[2]*

---

[2] Vern McLellan, *Quips, Quotes, and Quests* (Eugene, Oregon: Harvest House Publishers, 1982), 12.

2

A PREPARED HEART
Shaping Attitudes

Memory Verse: Ps. 27:8

The young couple dressed handsomely to meet the realtor at ten o'clock. "I wonder what the house is like and if he thinks we can afford it," the excited wife asked.

"I'm concerned about the septic system and the lot dimensions," her husband replied.

"Oh, how can you be so preoccupied with practical things?" she teased. "I want to know all about the schools, and if the neighbors are nice."

They made the ten-mile trip in silence, each contemplating the myriad questions and thoughts racing through their minds.

The smiling realtor greeted them immediately upon their arrival. "You're going to love this house," he assured them. "It has everything you want, plus it's in your price range."

They drove to the site in great anticipation and, just as the realtor had promised, it *was* wonderful. The couple flooded the real estate agent with questions as they weighed the pros and cons of the purchase, all the while hoping the answers would be what they wanted to hear.

Finally, the wife asked, "What about the neighbors? Are they friendly?"

"Well young lady, how friendly are the people in your present neighborhood?"

"Oh, they're wonderful friends," she answered.

"Then," countered the congenial salesman, "people in this vicinity will be too."

It's true! Our attitudes shape our outlook and actions. They make a difference in our attempt at living sacrificially. And, these attitudes are determined in large part by our focus.

Do you remember elementary art school classes? Our young minds easily grasped the fact that things far away appeared small and objects close to us seemed big. The same is true of God and his point of view. If we have our focus off of him and hold him far away, he will appear small and incapable and his ways will look foolish to us. However, if we are near to him, he will emerge as big and capable as he is in reality, and knowing him and his ways will be our priority.

We will be prepared to lay down our lives like Christ to the degree that we focus our hearts on God.

DISCOVERY 1: THE CHOICES OF FOCUS

1. Read Ps. 40:4. What three kinds of people are mentioned:

a. _____

b. _____

c. _____

The Hebrew definitions in that verse are as follows: *Trust* comes from the word *mibtach* meaning "confidence or security."[1] *Proud* comes from the word *rahab* meaning "defiant."[2] *Falsehood* comes from the word *kazab* meaning "a deceptive thing or a lie."[3]

Those who make God their confidence and security depend on him. Those who turn to the proud either say "There is no God" or "I don't need him." And, those who lapse into falsehood are trying to deceive God. Stated simply, we have three choices: Depend, Deny, or Deceive.

2. Look up at least two of the following verses and explain why deception doesn't work (Ps. 139:1–6, 52:3–5, 81:15; Jer. 17:9–10; Isa. 29:13–16; Job 15:31; Rom. 1:22–23). ____

____

3. Refer to at least two of the references below to see why defying God and denying him doesn't work (Ps. 28:5, 14:1; Titus 1:15–16; Jer. 6:16–19, 13:10–11, 17:5–6; Rom. 1:28–32). ____

____

4. Consult at least two of the verses below. Why or why not is dependence on God the wise choice? (James 4:8–10; John 14:21; Isa. 30:18; Ps. 31:19–20, 1:2–3, 91:14–16, 34:1–10; Heb. 11:6) ____

____

DISCOVERY 2: I CAN DEPEND ON GOD

We know that God wants us to depend on him and that there are great rewards for such action.

---

[1] Robert L. Thomas, gen. ed., *New American Standard Exhaustive Concordance of the Bible* (Nashville: Holman, 1981), 1543.

[2] Ibid., 1595.

[3] Ibid., 1536.

1. a. According to John 6:44 and Jer. 24:7, where do we get our ability to depend on him? _____

b. Read Deut. 6:4–6 and Jer. 29:13. How much of us does God want dependent on him? _____

c. Why or why not is it out of reach for us to do that, according to Deut. 30:9–11? _____

d. What is *God's way* to dependence on him, according to John 14:6? _____

Most of us will give assent to God's desire that we depend on him, for we believe that it is for our ultimate good. Some, however, will balk at God's way, since it seems intolerant to believe that there is only *one* way. Some readers may not as yet know Jesus personally. They may know about him, but have not experienced the assurance that he is a personal God who died on the cross for them. Not all may recognize, at this time, that we all desperately need a savior.

Certainly, living sacrificially would be of interest to "do-gooders" who are working their way into heaven. To give as God intended by laying down our lives for others, however, we must know *him*. We must be born again into the relationship that bridges the gap between our sinfulness and God's holiness. No amount of effort on our part is good enough. Without accepting Jesus as the only way to that reconciled relationship with God, our giving would have no power. The effort would eventually be short-circuited and frustration would follow; the follower may even fall away from Christian precepts.

Read John 3 and follow the progression below to see how you can make or reconfirm the most important decision of your life—to depend on God by accepting the work of Jesus Christ on your behalf.

2. Reread John 3:3. Express what the *need* is. _____

_____

3. Reread John 3:7. What *command* is given? _____

_____

4. Reread John 3:16. What is God's *plan* to fulfill the need and the command? _____

5. Reread John 3:19–20. What is the *natural condition* described? _____

6. Reread John 3:21. How is *conversion* described? _____

_____

7. a. Reread John 3:30. What practical advice is given for your spiritual *walk*—for subsequent, continuing dependence on God? _____

b. Where are you in that progression? _____

8. Do you love darkness rather than light? (Even in some areas of your life?) If so, in what areas? _____

_____

9. Do you see that you need the Savior in your life? _____

_____

10. a. Do you recognize God's plan to save from sin? _____

b. How does it apply to you? _____

_____

11. When did you come into the light? _____

12. How are you daily seeking to decrease as Jesus increases? _____

_____

13. a. Matt. 11:27–30 and Heb. 10:22–25 give wise counsel for practical ways that we can decrease as Jesus increases. What advice is especially helpful for you to persevere in depending on God? _____

_____

b. How would this help us lay down our lives for others?

_____

_____

DISCOVERY 3: THE STRUGGLE OF SELFISHNESS VS. SELFLESSNESS

Read Rom. 7–8, then reread Rom. 7:12–24.

1. What one word describes Paul's condition? _____

_____

2. a. How many times do the words *I, me,* and *my* appear in those ten verses? _____

b. Do you think it is correct to say that a focus on self produces struggle? Why or why not? _____

c. Where is the focus? _____

_____

3. Read Rom. 8:37. What one word describes the believer's situation? _____

4. a. How many times do the words *God, Christ, Lord, Jesus, him, Spirit, he, Son,* and *Father* appear in Rom. 7:25–8:39? _____

b. Do you think it correct to state that a focus on God produces victory? Why or why not? _____

_____

5. a. Where do you want your focus to be? _____

   b. How do you think your choice will prepare your heart for living sacrificially? _____

_____

DISCOVERY 4: ATTITUDES THAT DEVELOP A PREPARED HEART

Read the references that follow the heart illustration below to find twenty godly attitudes that will prepare us to give God's way, to love as he loves by laying down our lives. Record your one-word answers on a piece of paper.

A PREPARED HEART

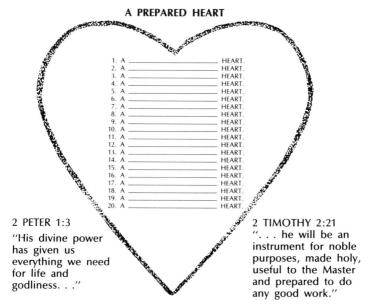

1. A _____ HEART.
2. A _____ HEART.
3. A _____ HEART.
4. A _____ HEART.
5. A _____ HEART.
6. A _____ HEART.
7. A _____ HEART.
8. A _____ HEART.
9. A _____ HEART.
10. A _____ HEART.
11. A _____ HEART.
12. A _____ HEART.
13. A _____ HEART.
14. A _____ HEART.
15. A _____ HEART.
16. A _____ HEART.
17. A _____ HEART.
18. A _____ HEART.
19. A _____ HEART.
20. A _____ HEART.

2 PETER 1:3

"His divine power has given us everything we need for life and godliness. . ."

2 TIMOTHY 2:21

". . . he will be an instrument for noble purposes, made holy, useful to the Master and prepared to do any good work."

   1. James 1:22–25; 1 John 3:18; John 14:31b; Neh. 9:15
   2. Isa. 33:6; 1 Tim. 3:13; 1 John 5:11–15; John 14:27

3. Prov. 4:23, 12:24, 27; Rom. 12:11; Heb. 6:10–11
4. 1 Tim. 4:8; Heb. 12:11–13; Prov. 23:12
5. 1 Thess. 5:11; Heb. 10:24–25, 3:13; 2 Cor. 1:3–4; Rom. 1:12, 15:5; Col. 2:2
6. 1 Thess. 5:18; Col. 2:7; Heb. 12:28
7. James 4:10; Matt. 23:12; 1 Peter 5:5–6; Isa. 66:2
8. Ps. 63:7, 16:11, 21:6, 33:1; John 17:13
9. John 13:34–35, 15:12–13; 1 John 3:16, 4:19; 2 Cor. 5:14
10. Matt. 4:4; Deut. 8:3; John 6:35; 2 Tim. 3:16–17; Heb. 4:12
11. 1 Sam. 15:22; 2 Cor. 10:13 TLB; Deut. 28:1; John 14:21, 15:10
12. Gal. 1:10; Matt. 5:8; James 4:8b; Prov. 21:2; 2 Tim. 2:22
13. Ps. 46:10, 131:2, 23:2; Isa. 30:15; 1 Peter 3:4
14. 1 Thess. 5:14, 2:8; Eph. 4:32
15. Phil. 2:3–4; Mark 10:45; Josh. 24:15; Luke 22:26–27
16. Gal. 6:9–10; 1 Cor. 15:58; Matt. 25:21; Luke 16:10; James 1:2–3; Heb. 12:12–13; 2 Tim. 4:7–9
17. Isa. 40:28–31; 2 Cor. 9:8, 3:5, 12:9–10; Ps. 73:26; 1 Peter 4:11
18. Ps. 86:11; Deut. 6:5; Jer. 29:13
19. Phil. 2:13; Isa. 6:8; 1 Chron. 28:9; Ps. 51:12, 54:6; John 7:17
20. Ps. 90:12; Prov. 24:5; James 3:17

To maintain these attitudes in readiness, remember to keep looking up to God in both the little and the big things of life. When God asks you to seek his face, tell him "Your face, LORD, I will seek" (Ps. 27:8).

DISCOVERY 5: APPLICATION

1. In what ways do you try to deceive God? _____

_____

2. How have you denied God? _____

_____

3. How have you defied him—by turning your back on him? _____

_____

4. In what specific ways will you depend on God today?

_____

5. a. Of the twenty heart attitudes mentioned, which ones are your strongest? _____

 b. Your weakest? _____

 c. What will you do to strengthen the feeble areas? _____

_____

A Parting Thought

"For the eyes of the LORD range
   throughout the earth
to strengthen those whose hearts
   are fully committed to him."

—2 Chron. 16:9a

3

ONE-WAY TRAFFIC. YIELD!
Being a Yielder

Memory Verse: Eph. 5:21

The car was hauled to a tractor-trailer lot. I watched the men try to unload it, but it wouldn't budge. "Can't git this durn thing to move off'n the flatbed, Charlie."

In the next instant I saw the Virginia mechanic slap his laugh-wrinkled forehead in comprehension and with a loud hoot he yelled, "Course! Had to put it in neutral!" And with that, the vehicle slid smoothly off the trailer bed and into the yard.

That amusing picture brightened my discouraged thoughts while flashing yellow lights jarred me back to reality. The grizzled, toothless mechanic offered me a bouncy ride to the nearest telephone where I called my husband about the breakdown, and the not-so-bright prognosis from the diesel experts.

Like the vehicle on the flatbed trailer, we don't go in God's direction until we get out of our own gear. Momentum in a believer's life requires getting into neutral and deferring to God's direction. It is imperative for us to get into his gear.

When we're willing to yield, we lay down our lives for others, voluntarily limiting our freedom so that God's best plan can be accomplished.

DISCOVERY 1: YIELDING TO GOD AND OTHERS

1. Look up the following three words in your dictionary:

a. Yield _____

b. Submit _____

c. Defer _____

2. What command is given in Eccl. 12:13? _____

3. a. According to Deut. 4:10 and 31:12, is the ability to fear God natural or is it learned? _____

b. How is it accomplished? _____

_____

4. a. To fear God means to reverence him. Read James 4:7–8 and 1 Peter 5:6. How do we best show God that we reverence him? _____

b. What are some of the benefits mentioned in Ps. 128 for one who fears the Lord? _____

_____

5. Read 2 Chron. 30:8. What four demands does God make?

a. _____

b. _____

c. _____

d. _____

6. a. In what area of your life are you giving stiff resistance to God? _____

_____

b. What can you do specifically to yield to him in that area? _____

_____

7. a. Read 2 Cor. 5:14–15. What should control us? _____

b. If something controls us, do we usually resist or surrender to it? _____

c. Is it possible to go through the motions of surrender but resist on the inside? _____

d. Give specifics from your experience. _____

_____

8. a. Why should we allow Christ's love to control us? _____

_____

b. What is the result of this yielding? _____

9. Read Eph. 5:21 and Phil. 2:3–4. After you have yielded to God, whom can you yield to next? How? _____

_____

DISCOVERY 2: WHAT IT MEANS TO YIELD

Look up the following verses and write down what you discover it means to yield or submit to others.

1. Gal. 5:13 _____

2. 1 Cor. 9:19 _____

3. 2 Cor. 4:5 _____

4. Rom. 8:5b _____

5. Rom. 15:1–2 _____

6. Rom. 12:10 _____

7. Rom. 14:19 _____

DISCOVERY 3: WHAT I CAN YIELD

Look up the following verses that tell *what* we can yield. Record your answers on the yield sign that follows.

1. Prov. 19:11
2. 2 Tim. 1:7; 2 Cor. 7:5
3. Amos 6:1
4. 1 Cor. 10:23
5. 2 Cor. 10:5
6. Eph. 4:26, 31
7. Eph. 4:29
8. Eph. 5:16
9. 1 Tim. 6:10
10. 1 John 2:17; Rom. 12:2
11. 1 Peter 5:5–6; Rom. 12:3; 1 Cor. 10:12
12. 1 Cor. 7:25
13. Rom. 14:1; 1 Cor. 10:31
14. Rom. 14:13
15. Matt. 6:34
16. Eccl. 8:5–6
17. Lev. 19:18; Deut. 32:35–36
18. Phil. 4:11–12

19. Matt. 19:16–22

20. Others?

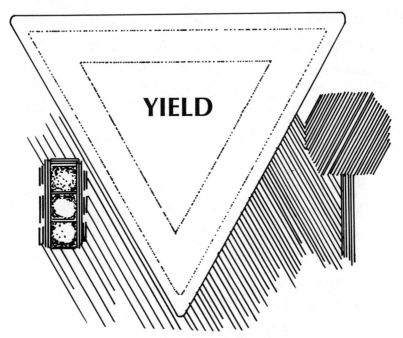

DISCOVERY 4: THE WARNINGS GOD GIVES

God is pleased when we consent to lay down ourselves for his interests. However, there are some warnings that should not be ignored. Look up the verses below to see what cautions are advised.

1. Prov. 28:21; 1 Tim. 5:21; James 2:8–9 _____

_____

2. Acts 4:36–5:5 _____

3. Col. 3:22–24 _____

DISCOVERY 5: WHAT TO LEARN FROM MARY'S JOSEPH

Let's learn to be yielders by observing what guideposts Mary's Joseph followed. We know that Joseph faced an impossible situation. Travel back in time to just a few months before the birth of Christ.

Plans were going ahead smoothly. There would not be too many guests, but enough to make the wedding festive. "The period of engagement is too long," Joseph complained to a friend, "and Mary seems so quiet lately."

"Bride's jitters," assured his friend.

Still Joseph could not dismiss the nagging uneasiness he felt.

Then the bomb hit. Mary told him some incredible things. He thought he knew her well, but now she seemed like a stranger.

Read Matt. 1:18–25.

STOP!

1. Review the facts Joseph was listing in his head. (Use vv. 18–19 to help you.) _____

_____

LISTEN!

2. God is speaking. Look at the facts from the Lord's point of view in vv. 20–21. _____

_____

3. What fact about Joseph in v. 19 explains why he would choose to listen to God? _____

4. a. How do vv. 22–23 give credibility to the angel's message? _____

   b. Why would Joseph know about that prophecy? _____

_____

YIELD!

   5. a. Review v. 19 again. What did Joseph want to do? ____

_____

_____

   b. What did the Lord tell him to do in v. 20? _____

_____

   c. According to v. 24, what did Joseph decide to do? ___

_____

   6. a. In what way does v. 25 indicate that Joseph deferred even further for God's best plan? _____

_____

_____

   b. How was that obedient action remarkable for a young, newly married man? _____

_____

   c. How do Matt. 2:13–22 and Luke 2:33, 39–52 indicate that Joseph continued to protect the child? _____

_____

_____

DISCOVERY 6: APPLICATION

   1. In what ways am I resistant to God? Why? _____

_____

2. In what ways am I surrendered? Why? _____

_____

_____

3. Check the things that are, personally, the hardest to yield.

Personal Yielding Chart

My rights ___	My thoughts ___	My anger ___
My words ___	My time ___	My money ___
My will ___	My position ___	My plans ___
My opinions ___	My judgments ___	My timing ___
Others' rights ___	My problems ___	My vengeance ___
My circumstances ___	My possessions ___	

Other things _____

4. a. To what persons in my life is it easiest to yield? Why?

_____

b. Hardest? Why? _____

_____

5. Write the names of the persons you live with on the lines below. In what ways could you yield to them to make them more complete in God's design?

_____

_____

6. Think of a situation that requires immediate yielding. Go through the three steps Joseph employed to set himself aside and defer to God's plan in Mary's life.

a. STOP. Review the facts from your point of view.

_____

b. LISTEN. See the facts from God's point of view.

c. YIELD. Obey God's direction.

Maybe God has in mind a direction for your life, which is totally different from your own plan. How will you specifically obey him? _____

_____

_____

A Parting Thought

"The hardest thing to give is in."[1]

---

[1] E. C. McKenzie, *14,000 Quips and Quotes for Writers and Speakers* (New York: Greenwich House, 1984), 205.

4

FORGERY OR ORIGINAL MASTERPIECE?
Being Vulnerable

Memory Verse: 2 Cor. 3:16

Authentic things are treasured possessions. An original painting by Rembrandt is worth much more than its forged counterpart; antiques bring a higher price than their reproductions. *You* are a treasured possession to God (Deut. 26:18) and he is interested in an authentic you—the you who is open, honest, and vulnerable. He is patient but not pleased with masks that have to be painstakingly chipped away. And he is especially displeased with Sunday Christians who won't live their faith every day.

Do you remember the Lone Ranger and Tonto? After the struggle was over and all had recognized and appreciated the good deed, the white horse carried its master off into the sunset. The narrator's voice would follow the galloping dust and ask, "Who was that masked man?" The Lone Ranger lived up to the good code of the West but hid a part of himself from all his viewers. He was captivating and mysterious, but what was he hiding?

Charles Swindoll has said "authentic people usually enjoy life more than most. They don't take themselves so seriously. They actually laugh and cry and think more freely because they have nothing to prove—no big image to protect, no role to play. They have no fear of being found out, because they're not hiding anything."[1]

God created a unique and beautiful you. But are you a forgery of yourself, like a copy of a grand masterpiece? Let's learn together how to effectively strip away the masks in our lives. We can lay down our lives by looking to the Lord, shedding our cover-ups, and becoming a mirror image of God.

DISCOVERY 1: VULNERABILITY

Note the following definition.

> "Vulnerability: the capability of being wounded; being liable to greater penalties or bonuses."[2]

1. Look up the following verses and describe what it means to be vulnerable.

a. Heb. 4:13 _____

b. 2 Cor. 6:11–13 _____

c. John 3:20–21 _____

d. Acts 28:30–31 _____

e. Esther 2:14 _____

f. Eph. 3:13–15 _____

---

[1] Charles Swindoll, *Strengthening Your Grip* (Waco, Texas: Word Books, 1982), 22–23.

[2] *Webster's New Collegiate Dictionary*, 958.

DISCOVERY 2: HOW OTHERS WILL RESPOND

1. According to Ps. 139:1–16, what does God know about me? _____

_____

2. What does God focus on, according to 1 Sam. 16:7? ___

_____

3. Read 2 Cor. 5:21. What potential does God see for me?

_____

4. a. Read Rom. 8:1–4. Does God condemn me, the believer, since he knows 100% of me? _____

b. Why or why not? _____

_____

5. According to Rom. 5:8–10 and Jer. 31:3–4, of what can I be assured as I expose myself to God? _____

_____

6. a. According to Rom. 8:5b and 2 Cor. 5:14–17, how will yielded Christian disciples choose to look at me? _____

_____

b. Why? _____

_____

7. Read Rom. 8:5a and 1 Cor. 2:14. How will some nonbelievers see me? _____

8. What comfort can I get from Ps. 56:4, 118:6, and Heb. 13:6? _____

_____

DISCOVERY 3: LEARNING FROM NEHEMIAH

Read Nehemiah 1 for the background to this story.

Nehemiah straightened the towel on his arm as he prepared the wine carafe for the king's table. Preoccupied, he spilled a drop on the floor. He couldn't get the recent conversation with his brother out of his mind. "I can't believe the Jews in Jerusalem are having so much trouble," he said to himself, choking back tears when he thought about the report of the broken walls and the charred gates swinging aimlessly on half-melted hinges.

"Oh God," he prayed, "I have fasted for days and I cry when I am reminded of the sin of my people, but you have redeemed us. As your servant, Lord, I beg you to listen to me."

Duty called and Nehemiah—the man whose name meant "God has consoled"—put aside his emotions in order to be faithful to the king. He returned to his task of pouring wine at the lavish, royal table.

Answer the following questions, using the verses listed to help you see how Nehemiah became vulnerable.

1. What was Nehemiah's special job (Neh. 1:11)? _____

2. According to v. 11, what indication do you see that Nehemiah had planned to be vulnerable with the king?

_____

3. What kind of attitude was normal for Nehemiah to have before the king (Neh. 2:1b)? _____

4. What did the king notice about Nehemiah this time (Neh. 2:2)?

_____

5. According to 2:2, what emotion was Nehemiah experiencing? _____

6. Did that stop Nehemiah from telling the king what was making him sad? _____

7. What in 2:3 indicates that Nehemiah showed respect for the king? _____

8. a. According to 2:3, what did Nehemiah say was the reason for his sadness? _____

   b. According to the background given in Chapter 1, was Nehemiah honest in his response? _____

   c. Did Nehemiah tell the king all the details of Israel's sin? _____

   d. Why was it unnecessary to share all the details? _____

_____

9. What did Nehemiah do quickly before answering the king's request in 2:4? _____

10. What was Nehemiah's plan? _____

11. What was the king's response? _____

_____

12. a. According to 2:6–8, what concessions did Nehemiah and the king make to help each other? _____

_____

   b. How do these concessions indicate that neither man was trying to manipulate the other? _____

13. According to 2:8, why did the king grant Nehemiah's requests? _____

14. a. How did God answer Nehemiah's prayer, as recorded in 1:11? _____

b. How do you think God blesses us when we are open with others? _____

_____

15. a. Upon arriving in Jerusalem, Nehemiah inspected the work and organized and implemented his plan to rebuild. Was the wall ever finished (6:15–16)? _____

b. How was it accomplished? _____

Nehemiah employed ten principles in his openness.

1. He chose to be vulnerable.

2. He prayed for success.

3. He faced his fear.

4. He had respect for his listener.

5. He was honest but careful.

6. He prayed again.

7. He had a plan. (He wasn't just rehearsing a problem to get pity.)

8. He didn't manipulate his listener.

9. He was considerate.

10. He recognized that God blessed his vulnerability.

DISCOVERY 4: THE RISKS INVOLVED

1. Read the following verses in Nehemiah and note what this diligent leader faced as a result of his vulnerability.

a. Neh. 2:2 _____

b. Neh. 2:10 _____

c. Neh. 4:1–4 _____

d. Neh. 4:10 _____

2. According to Neh. 4:4, how did Nehemiah handle ridicule? _____

3. a. How did he handle displeasure and anger (see Neh. 4:9)? _____

   b. According to Prov. 2:11, how can we guard against worrying about the anger and displeasure of others? _____

_____

   c. How does Phil. 4:6–7 help us in this regard? _____

_____

4. a. How did Nehemiah handle fear (Neh. 4:14)? _____

_____

   b. Look at 2 Tim. 1:7. What three things can we exchange our fear for? _____

5. a. How did Nehemiah handle discouragement and weakness (Neh. 4:6, 17)? _____

   b. What weapons do we have at our disposal (Eph. 6:10–18)? _____

DISCOVERY 5: BEING VULNERABLE IN EVERYDAY LIVING

Look up each of the verses on the following mask and meditate on them. On another piece of paper, record how the verses apply to you. (You might want to use a pencil to trace the mask onto another piece of paper. As you review each verse, erase that part of the mask, until all sections of the cover-up are gone.)

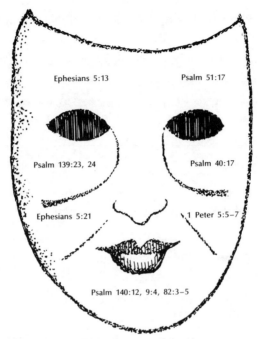

Ephesians 5:13   Psalm 51:17

Psalm 139:23, 24   Psalm 40:17

Ephesians 5:21   1 Peter 5:5–7

Psalm 140:12, 9:4, 82:3–5

DISCOVERY 6: RESPONDING TO THOSE WHO ARE OPEN

Go back to Nehemiah 4 for some answers.

1. According to v. 13, at what points of the wall did Nehemiah station the people? _____

_____

2. In what manner were the people stationed at the exposed places? _____

_____

When someone is vulnerable, the family of God must be dependable, stationed right at the exposed places, armed appropriately with the Word, a prayer, a hug, a listening ear, encouragement, and commitment to keep a confidence, allowing no gossip.

Will *you* do that?

DISCOVERY 7: APPLICATION

1. Circle the risks of vulnerability that are hardest for you to overcome: ridicule, fear, discouragement, anger of others, weakness. Something else? _____

2. Have you ever been deeply hurt because you had been vulnerable? What happened? _____

_____

_____

3. What persons do you feel you could be most vulnerable with? _____

4. Why would it not be right to be vulnerable with just anyone? _____

_____

5. When do you feel the most unguarded and exposed?

_____

_____

6. a. Do you know an area in your life now where you need to be more vulnerable? How could you apply Nehemiah's ten principles in order to become more vulnerable? __

_____

_____

b. Will you pray about it? _____

_____

A Parting Thought

Revelation

We make ourselves a place apart
    Behind light words that tease and flout,
But oh, the agitated heart
    Till someone find us really out.

'Tis pity if the case require
    (or so we say) that in the end
We speak the literal to inspire
    The understanding of a friend.

But so with all, from babes that play
    At hide-and-seek to God afar,
So all who hide too well away
    Must speak and tell us where they are.[3]

—Robert Frost

5

EARNING THE TITLE: DIPLOMAT
Being a Peacemaker: The First To Reconcile

Memory Verse: Rom. 12:18

Have you ever wanted to be first at something—anything? Have you imagined yourself running a victory lap to the wild cheers of an enthusiastic crowd? Have you fantasized about receiving congratulations from the president of the United States for being the only person who could bring two warring nations together?

It's exhilarating to be first when everyone notices our achievements; it's great to be the best in things that we want to do. Who wouldn't want to be first at achieving the "impossible"? Down deep, we'd all love to win a tough race or a blue ribbon at the fair.

But, what about being first in difficult things or at those times when no one is applauding? Mother Teresa ignored risks and literally embraced hundreds of lepers. It didn't matter that it wouldn't be easy, that she may not have wanted to do it, or that she might not have an audience.

Even though it might be difficult, do you still want to be first at something? Now it's possible! You can be the first to reconcile in any situation. In the New Testament, we see that Zacchaeus worked at reconciliation when he hurt others and, in the Old Testament, we read that Joseph took the initiative when *he* was the one offended. They were both diplomats, laying down their lives for others. You can be a reconciler, too, changing yourself first, whether you are the offender or the offended.

DISCOVERY 1: THE CHARACTER QUALITIES OF A PEACEMAKER

In his book, *Improving Your Serve,* Charles Swindoll suggests several character qualities that a peacemaker should possess. A peacemaker:

1. is at peace with one's self

2. works hard to settle quarrels, not start them

3. is accepting and tolerant

4. takes no pleasure in being negative

5. builds others up

6. purposes to heal rather than hurt

7. is slow to anger

8. "is humble and trusting."[1]

Another to add to the list is that a peacemaker is:

9. pure and sincere in personal relationships.

These qualities are important for any diplomat to pursue.

---

[1] Charles R. Swindoll, *Improving Your Serve* (Waco, Texas: Word Books, 1981), 118–19.

DISCOVERY 2: LEARNING FROM DIPLOMATS ZACCHAEUS AND JOSEPH

Read Luke 19:1–10.

1. Who was Zacchaeus? _____

_____

2. Was Zacchaeus the one offended, or did he offend others (vv. 2, 8)? _____

3. a. Whom did he want to see? _____

b. When Zacchaeus saw the one he longed to see, what was Zacchaeus's response (v. 6)? _____

4. Why did Jesus' visit to Zacchaeus's home make Zacchaeus want to reconcile with others (vv. 8, 10)? _____

_____

5. a. What were the results in Zacchaeus's life when he made things right with the people he had wronged (v. 9)? ___

b. Did it cost Zacchaeus anything, and if so, what? _____

c. How was it worth it? _____

_____

Read Genesis 45 aloud and consider the background to the story, as described below.

Joseph was a favorite among many sons, but he alienated others in his family and they plotted his demise. His jealous brothers threw the youngster into a pit where they would have left him as prey for wild animals, robbers, bad weather, and starvation. Such a plan was worse than death: separation from family, favor, comfort, and security. But because of the conscience of one among them, and because they did not wish blood on their hands, the greedy brothers bargained with the worst sort of marauding traders. They sold Joseph into slavery.

Through God's favor, and Joseph's abilities and natural charisma, Joseph wooed the Egyptian authorities. After desperate struggles with loneliness, betrayal, imprisonment, and neglect, he became a respected advisor in Pharaoh's court.

Now the guilty brothers arrive in Egypt—years later—needing help to survive the famine in their land. Would Joseph put himself back in the pit, emotionally, at the first sight of them? Or, would Joseph be a willing diplomat, allowing God to help him reach for reconciliation? All Joseph had been guilty of was immature boasting and "bugging" his brothers with his dreams—that was it. His brothers were the offenders and they hurt him badly.

What would you do? (For guidance, read Ps. 40:1–2.)

Take a second look at Genesis 45, and answer the following questions to discover eight principles Joseph used to reconcile with his brothers.

1. In what frame of mind did Joseph approach his brothers? Was he open and honest with his emotions or was he closed and deceptive (vv. 1–2)? _____

2. Did Joseph list facts or speculations of the offense (v. 4)?

_____

3. Did Joseph treat his offenders with comfort or condemnation (v. 5)? _____

4. Whose purpose did Joseph try to see in it all (v. 5)? _____

5. To whom did Joseph give the credit for his being in Egypt (vv. 8–9)? _____

6. a. When telling his story to his brothers, did Joseph act mired in the petty details? _____

b. What specific issues did Joseph focus on (vv. 3, 13, and 19)? _____

_____

7. What is Joseph's desire in vv. 10 and 11? _____

_____

8. a. Did Joseph accomplish reconciliation (vv. 14–15)? __

b. What were the results (vv. 20, 27)? _____

_____

DISCOVERY 3: HOW TO BE AN AMBASSADOR

Reconciliation is a ministry. Joseph and Zacchaeus were members of the eternal diplomatic corps—and we can be too. Because of our relationship with Jesus Christ, each of us could have car licenses that boast "diplomat" preceding the number of our vehicle registration. In 2 Cor. 5:14–21, Paul gives us a prestigious title. We are "Christ's ambassadors." We have a mandate for reconciliation with Christ and mankind. Certainly, our right relationship with God the Father motivates us to maintain unity and peace with all people. The Spirit's power accomplishes it in a willing servant. We need to reach out to believers—cohorts in the corps—and to those who aren't as quick to see the need to be reconciled.

1. What is our motivation in diplomacy (2 Cor. 5:14)? ____

2. What is our pattern in diplomacy (2 Cor. 5:15)? _____

_____

3. What instruction is given to reconcilers (2 Cor. 5:16–18)? _____

_____

4. What is the diplomat's message (2 Cor. 5:19–21)? _____

_____

_____

DISCOVERY 4: WHEN RECONCILIATION ATTEMPTS FAIL

Tina's trembling hand reached for the telephone. It had been surprisingly silent all morning, giving her time alone with Jesus, and she knew she had to call her friend to apologize. Tina dialed the familiar number and waited. . . . Finally a voice answered on the other end.

"Hello. Nancy, this is Tina," she croaked. Was Tina imagining it? Nancy's tone was distant and the returned "hello" was abrupt. "Nancy, I need to get right to the point. I know I have offended you and I want to ask your forgiveness." Tina surprised herself by breaking the ensuing silence with a second overture. "It was wrong of me to take the praise you deserved for the committee work, especially after not completing my jobs on time. I know I caused you extra work and worry. Please forgive me."

In the awkward pause that followed, Tina prayed for the right words. She longed to be embraced with the words: "It's all right. I've done it myself before and I'm sure we'll work better together next time." Those words didn't come. All that returned through the now sweaty receiver was a stony silence.

"Nancy? Are you still there?"

"Yes," came the cool, flat response.

"Nancy . . . will you please forgive me?"

"Yes!" she hissed, and hung up.

Tina sat with her mouth open in astonishment and then quickly became annoyed. Nancy had said yes, but Tina's heart wasn't comforted. The guilt remained and the hurt cut deeper.

Tina's heart pounded the next time she saw Nancy walking into church. Her pace was brisk; her face tired. Tina hurried to catch up to her. Nancy seemed taller than ever. (They had laughed often about their differences in height.) Nancy's shoulders stiffened as Tina called her name and Tina was now sure of the wall between them. The barbed wire separating them was now electrified and sparks of hate flew from Nancy's eyes as Tina said, "Would you consider meeting me after church? I'd like a few minutes with you if I could." Her response was an echo of the loud silence of a few days earlier.

Tina didn't hear much of the sermon that morning. She spanked her conscience over and over. "I'm so stupid! I could have finished that work for her. There's no excuse. And, when the pastor thanked *me* for the job well done, I should have given *her* all the credit. That's a character flaw of mine. I'm too impressed with praise. And, how dumb to *call* her to apologize. I should have gone to her house right away. And, maybe I shouldn't have rushed her today."

The last "amen" called Tina's attention back to the worship service. She wanted to go home, put on her bathrobe, stuff her mouth with candy, and cry into the newspaper, but she decided to run after Nancy one more time. When Tina reached the parking lot, Nancy's car wasn't there.

Tina's thoughts were absorbed with this problem for days. She flogged herself while making lunches for the children. While making beds, she practiced new approaches to seek forgiveness. While driving the carpool, she corrected Nancy in her mind for her unforgiving spirit. Every time Tina read the Bible it seemed to point to the differences that she had caused. Calls to Nancy resulted in her husband repeatedly saying: "She isn't home." At church Tina seemed always to catch glimpses of Nancy's car's taillights. At Bible study, icy stares returned Tina's weak smiles and it wasn't long before Nancy didn't come to church at all anymore.

Tina decided to tell a mature Christian friend about this problem and ask that they go together to see Nancy. They went. They were rebuffed. The only long string of words from Nancy came in the detailed outlining of Tina's offenses. They were all true and Tina squirmed under the weight of them.

1. a. Review Rom. 12:18, the memory verse for this lesson. "If it is possible, as far as it depends on you, live at peace with everyone." What does the phrase "if it is possible" imply? _____

_____

  b. What does "as far as it depends on you" mean? _____

_____

2. What steps did Tina take to reconcile with Nancy? _____

_____

3. What indicates that Tina consulted with the Lord before going to her friend? _____

_____

4. How did Nancy respond? _____

5. a. What did Tina do right? _____

_____

  b. What did Tina do wrong? _____

_____

6. a. What did Nancy do right? _____

_____

b. What did Nancy do wrong? _____

_____

7. Did Tina do all she could to make things right with Nancy? _____

_____

8. Did Tina fulfill her responsibility? If so, at what point? __

_____

9. If Tina came to you for advice after all she had done, what could you give her from Rom. 12:10–21 and James 5:7–11? _____

_____

DISCOVERY 5: APPLICATION

1. Recall the character qualities of a peacemaker. Decide which are easy for you and which are difficult. Make checks in the proper columns below and determine what you will do about the findings of your self-analysis.

A Peacemaker:	Easy	Difficult
A. Is at peace with oneself		
B. Works hard to settle quarrels, not start them		
C. Is accepting and tolerant (an acceptor, not an exceptor;		
D. Takes no pleasure in being negative		
E. Is humble and trusting, taking God's strength as personal strength		

A Peacemaker:	Easy	Difficult
F. Builds others up G. Purposes to heal rather than hurt H. Is pure (sincere in relationships with others)		

Ask someone to pray about these findings with you. If you're in a group, perhaps the person sitting on your left could pray with you about your problem areas for at least a two-week period. See what God will do.

2. Do you take the ministry of reconciliation seriously in your own life? Recall examples. _____

_____

_____

3. a. Which of your relationships needs reconciling right now? _____

_____

b. Have you hurt that one or have they hurt you? _____

4. How is your present walk with the living God causing you to desire reconciliation with that one? _____

_____

5. If someone has hurt you, is one of those hurts still festering? Think of the persons involved and the situation. Go through each of the steps that Joseph utilized in diplomacy. Make the first move to reconcile with your offenders.

a. How can you be open and honest with your emotions? _____

b. List the facts, not the speculations of the offense. _____

_____

_____

c. How could you comfort your offender(s)? _____

_____

d. What might God's purpose be in it all? (This may require hindsight. It may be too early to know.) _____

_____

e. Find something positive in this situation. Can you give God the credit for the positive things? _____

_____

f. What are the really important issues in your situation?_

_____

g. How can you show your offender that you desire unity? _____

_____

h. What will you do to seek and obtain reconciliation? _

_____

i. As a result, what blessings of obedience might you enjoy? _____

_____

6. What attitude(s) can you change in yourself to facilitate reconciliation where needed? _____

_____

_____

A Parting Thought

"We are most like beasts when we kill.
We are most like men when we judge.
We are most like God when we forgive."[2]

[2] Lloyd Cory, ed., *Quotable Quotations* (Wheaton, Illinois: Victor Books, a division of Scripture Press Publications, Inc., 1985), 143.

6

DEFENDER OR PROSECUTOR?
Being a Peacemaker: A Wise Reprover

Memory Verse: Col. 1:28

Trial lawyers fall into one of two categories. They are either defenders or prosecutors. As we live under God's watchful eye, we too either come to the defense of those accused or heap complaints upon the defendants. It's been said that "Lawyers would have a hard time making a living if people behaved themselves and kept their promises."[1]

However, advocates of the law have one large fact of life in their favor. Human beings have difficulty conducting themselves properly and keeping true to their obligations. We are sinners and even if we can fool the world into thinking we're always upright, God knows better. We miss his target many times each day. We think amiss and we act amiss. That's one of the reasons God provided the Savior for

---

[1] E. C. McKenzie, *14,000 Quips and Quotes for Writers and Speakers* (New York: Baker Book House Company, Greenwich House, Crown Publishers, Inc., 1980), 295.

us and why he equipped us for the Christian fellowship that nurtures that relationship with Jesus. We need each other desperately.

When we tell another person about shortcomings we have discerned in their lives, we must remember two important facts:

1. Probably the fault we discern is something that person is already painfully aware of.

2. Most likely the reason we notice the weakness is because we ourselves have problems in that same area. The weaknesses that require reproof should not be quirks that annoy us, but things that are thorns to God, who is about the business of helping each of us become all we can be.

A wise reprover is a peacemaker, one who lays down his or her life by depending on God and keeping his interests in mind. Such a person paves the way for God to act, offering freedom for the offending one to change and grow in a way that pleases the Lord. The reprover's invitation should be sincere and under the authority of almighty God.

DISCOVERY 1: A DEFINITION AND COMMAND

1. Look up the following verses and formulate the motivation for, and the definition of, reproof.

a. Rom. 15:1–2 _____

b. 1 Thess. 4:9–10 _____

c. 2 Cor. 10:13 _____

d. Eph. 4:11–16 _____

e. Acts 18:26 _____

f. 2 Tim. 3:17 _____

g. Col. 1:28 _____

2. Read the verses below and determine what commands you are given.

    a. 2 Tim. 4:2 _____

    b. 1 Thess. 5:14–15 _____

    c. Matt. 18:12–14 _____

    d. 1 Tim. 5:20 _____

    e. Eph. 5:8–14a _____

DISCOVERY 2: PREREQUISITES TO WISE REPROOF

1. According to Gal. 6:1; Rom. 2:1, and Matt. 7:1–5 what must we realize about ourselves before attempting to reprove anyone else? _____

_____

2. Before we reprove someone, it is essential that we know God is asking us to do so. Our insight into problem areas may only be for the purpose of intercession. How will the guidance of 1 Thess. 5:17 help us determine if God is nudging us to reprove someone or not? _____

_____

_____

3. Another important prerequisite is mentioned in Eccl. 8:5–6. What should we give careful attention to? _____

_____

_____

4. What must our attitude be about *being* reproved (Prov. 10:17, 15:10, 32)? _____

_____

5. Look at Rom. 12:9–18. How do those verses indicate that we must build a relationship with the person—earning the right to be heard—*before* we reprove? _____

_____

_____

6. a. According to Prov. 15:2, what ingredient is absolutely necessary in order to speak knowledgeably? _____

_____

b. According to James 1:5, how do we get wisdom? ____

_____

c. Look at James 3:13–18. Fill in the chart below to get a picture of the two kinds of wisdom available to us.

Type of Wisdom	Characteristics	Results
Wisdom from the World		
Wisdom from God		

d. Which kind of wisdom do you want to characterize your life? _____

7. a. According to 2 Tim. 3:16–17 what four things does the Word of God—the Bible—offer?

1) _____

2) _____

3) _____

4) _____

b. What is the result in the man of God? _____

---

c. How would your effectiveness as a wise reprover suffer without being in God's Word regularly? _____

---

8. Read the prayer in John 17:21.

a. What did Jesus ask God for? _____

b. According to Col. 3:14, what is the perfect bond of unity? _____

c. What characteristics must we be developing to be able to reprove wisely (Col. 3:12–14)? _____

DISCOVERY 3: THE PURPOSE OF WISE REPROOF

Question: What is the scene?
Answer: A courtroom.
Question: Who are you?
Answer: One of the attorneys for the defense.
Question: Who is on trial?
Answer: A person in need of wise reproof.

The gavel hits hard upon the wood blocks, making you jump in your seat. Your heart is bouncing against the walls of your chest. The courtroom is full and every eye follows you. "All rise!" booms the bailiff.

1. According to James 4:12 and Isa. 33:22, who is the one lawgiver and judge? _____

2. Read 1 John 2:1. Who is the defender, or lawyer, for us all? _____

3. Who is our justifier (Rom. 8:33–34; Isa. 43:25)? _____

_____

4. a. Whose case are we arguing (Isa. 43:26)? _____

_____

b. Who is your partner on the defense team? _____

5. Will the verdict be "guilty" or "not guilty" for the offender (Rom. 3:23)? _____

6. What is the sentence for this crime (Rom. 6:23)? _____

_____

7. Who will carry out the sentence (Rom. 2:16, 5:8–9)? ___

_____

8. In Rom. 2:4 what does the kindness of God lead us to? _

_____

9. a. According to 2 Cor. 5:21, what potential does God see for the rehabilitated sinner? _____

_____

b. In one word, what is God interested in accomplishing (2 Cor. 5:18–20)? _____

10. Read the verses listed below and record on the following gavel diagram what our aim is in reproof.

a. Matt. 18:15; 2 Thess. 3:14–15 _____

b. Gal. 6:1 _____

c. 2 Cor. 5:18–20 _____

d. Acts 3:19 _____

e. Luke 22:32 _____

f. Titus 1:13 _____

g. Acts 18:23–26 _____

THE AIM OF REPROOF

a. _____   e. _____
b. _____   f. _____
c. _____   g. _____
d. _____

DISCOVERY 4: THE STEPS TO REPROOF

1. Read Matt. 18:15–17. If a sister or brother sins, to whom do you go

a. First? _____

b. Second? _____

c. Third? _____

DISCOVERY 5: LEARNING FROM NATHAN

1. *A Profile of Nathan*

a. Read 2 Sam. 7:1–17. Who was Nathan (v. 2)? _____

b. What did Nathan say to King David in v. 3? _____

c. What did God tell Nathan to tell David in vv. 4–16?

_____

d. According to v. 17, how was Nathan honorable to the Lord's message? _____

_____

e. How had Nathan earned the right to be heard by David? _____

_____

2. *A Look at David's Mistake*

　a. Read 2 Sam. 11.

　b. List David's many wrongdoings. _____

_____

_____

3. *Nathan's Reproof Examined*

　a. Read 2 Sam. 12. According to v. 1, whose idea was it for Nathan to rebuke David? _____

　b. Was Nathan obedient? _____

　c. What words would describe Nathan's approach in vv. 1b–4?

_____

　d. In what way did Nathan appeal to David's sense of justice? _____

_____

　e. What was David's response (vv. 5–6)? _____

_____

f. How do vv. 7–10, and 14 reveal how Nathan spelled out the gravity of the situation? What ramifications were there? _____

_____

g. How did Nathan lead David to realize that his sin was really against the Lord—not Bathsheba and Uriah alone (vv. 9, 10, 14)? _____

_____

h. How was Nathan careful to indicate what consequences would come from the sins (vv. 11–15, 19)? _____

_____

i. Verse 13 is very important. What admission did David make? _____

_____

j. How did Nathan give David freedom to confess and repent? _____

_____

k. What proclamation did Nathan make after David's confession? _____

_____

l. What happier circumstances brought Nathan to David the next time (vv. 24–25)? _____

_____

m. How was God's love affirmed to David via Nathan throughout the whole ordeal? _____

_____

_____

Note that Nathan's reproof of David was:

1. God's idea
2. Gentle
3. Wise
4. Direct

5. Complete
6. Serious
7. Consequential
8. Freeing

9. Reconciling
10. Loving

DISCOVERY 6: APPLICATION

1. What people do you accept reproof from most readily? Why? _____

_____

2. a. What were the specifics of a circumstance you know of where someone was reproved incorrectly? _____

_____

_____

b. What were the results? _____

_____

c. Describe a correct, loving reproof you are familiar with. _____

_____

_____

d. What were the results this time? _____

_____

3. What do you think the key ingredient is in the restoration of one who is in error? _____

4. If you are considering reproving someone, answer the following questions to discover what prerequisites you have accomplished and which ones you must still work on.

a. How have I been guilty of the same thing? _____

_____

b. Am I sure God wants me to say anything? _____

c. Is this the right time? _____

d. How did I respond the last time I was reproved? Was it a correct response in God's eyes? _____

_____

e. Have I earned the right to be heard? Have I developed a good relationship with the person I will reprove? _____

_____

f. How am I developing godly wisdom? _____

_____

g. Am I in God's Word consistently? _____

h. How am I allowing God to teach me holiness, compassion, kindness, humility, gentleness, patience, and forgiveness? _____

_____

5. Think again of the person God may be asking you to reprove. Examine the specifics by asking yourself the following questions.

a. Is it God's idea that I reprove this person, or is it mine? How can I be sure? _____

_____

_____

b. How can I be gentle? _____

_____

_____

_____

c. What would be a wise approach? _____

_____

_____

d. How can I be direct, yet tactful? _____

_____

_____

e. How can I communicate to the person all of the ramifications as I understand them? _____

_____

_____

f. In what way can I show how serious this is to God? ___

_____

_____

_____

g. What do I think the consequences might be? _____

_____

_____

_____

h. How can I give the person the freedom to agree with God? _____

_____

_____

_____

i. How can the person achieve reconciliation with God?

_____

j. How can the person reconcile with other people affected by the problem? _____

_____

k. In what ways can I show affirming love for the one being reproved? _____

_____

Now, pray about it again and again and do God's bidding.

A Parting Thought

"Confrontation plus caring brings growth
just as judgment plus grace brings salvation."[2]
—*Howard Clinebell, Jr.*

---

[2] David Augsburger, *Caring Enough to Confront* (Glendale, California: Regal Books, A Division of G/L Publications, 1980), 20.

7

THE TUG-OF-WAR
Being Committed to a Good Report

Memory Verse: Prov. 18:21

The speaker held an ordinary shoe box in his hands and had his audience spellbound. He had earlier declared that inside this plain box was the most deadly weapon in existence. People were silently guessing. Was it a specialized gun? Was it something nuclear? This weapon, he continued, had the potential for grave destruction. It could reduce even the most powerful of people to pygmies in stature. It could level whole ethnic groups at a single shot and render individuals defenseless against its mighty blows. He opened the box s-l-o-w-l-y, careful not to jiggle the contents. Was it a poisonous draft? A venomous snake? No! It was a large, slimy, altogether grotesque . . . tongue.

It's true. The speaker's box contained a cow's tongue, used to represent the human counterpart—a small vessel with great power. It can inflict damage or reflect love. Death or life! We offer quick verdicts and others either become the victims of our tongues or the beneficiaries of blessing from them. We can use our tongues for healing or hurting. The choice is ours and the proper option is to lay down our lives by being committed to a good report.

DISCOVERY 1: THE TONGUE'S IMPORTANCE

Look up the following Scripture references and note the three ways God describes the tongue.

1. James 3:3 likens the tongue to a _____.

2. James 3:4 sees the tongue as a _____.

3. James 3:5–6 pictures the tongue as a _____.

DISCOVERY 2: A GOOD REPORT

Giving a good report is a choice. It's choosing to think and say the best of someone or some situation, remembering that, when a critical attitude leads to a bad report, we've ignored the "one fact rule." That rule states that there is always *at least* one fact we don't know about someone else that would likely explain his or her behavior to our satisfaction.

Look up Phil. 4:8. What eight things does Paul tell us to let our minds dwell on?

1. "whatever is _____ "

2. "whatever is _____ "

3. "whatever is _____ "

4. "whatever is _____ "

5. "whatever is _____ "

6. "whatever is _____ "

7. "whatever is _____ "

8. "whatever is _____ "

Choosing to dwell on these eight attributes crowds out a bad report. When weighing the two options—a good report versus a bad report—keeping Phil. 4:8 in mind will push you on the side of a good report.

DISCOVERY 3: ELIZABETH WINS BY GIVING A GOOD REPORT

Read Luke 1:5–45 and you'll see that Elizabeth had a choice. She could have considered it a privilege to be with Mary (as she chose to do), or she could have accused and gossiped about the unwed girl with the preposterous story about a pending "virgin" birth.

Play Elizabeth's role from both sides. Act out Elizabeth encouraging Mary, and then, set up the drama as Elizabeth would have appeared if she had given a bad report. Put yourself in Elizabeth's shoes.

1. Reread Luke 1:41. What is the one variable that makes the difference between our choice to defend and bless or accuse and gossip? _____

_____

_____

_____

2. Consider Elizabeth's experience, and make a list of the good ways she used the tongue. For instance, we've already said that she encouraged Mary, so you could write "encouragement" on the top of the list.

Good Uses of the Tongue

    a. Encouragement

    b. _____

c. _____

d. _____

e. _____

f. _____

g. _____

h. _____

Any more?

3. Look up Luke 1:46–56, 66. How did Elizabeth's choice to fellowship with Mary and to choose a good report over a bad one affect Mary? Elizabeth's neighbors and relatives? ___

_____

_____

_____

_____

DISCOVERY 4: WHAT ENCOURAGES GOOD AND BAD REPORTS?

It's important to know what encourages good and bad reports so that we can pursue that which motivates us to do the right thing, and stay away from that which pulls us to the bad. It's like a tug-of-war. We need to choose which side we will pull on. Will you give attention to that which encourages a good report, or will you focus on that which motivates a bad one?

In the tug-of-war pictured in the following diagram, read each reference and decide what things encourage winning on either side of the rope, and how they contrast with each other. Finish the tug-of-war before going on to Discovery 5.

TUG-OF-WAR
Which Side is Winning in Your Life?

TEAM NUMBER ONE Pulling For What Will Encourage A GOOD REPORT.	TEAM NUMBER TWO Pulling For What Will Encourage A BAD REPORT.

1. _____
   Ephesians 5:1–13

2. _____
   Romans 8:5, 12:2;
   1 Peter 4:6

3. _____
   Philippians 4:8

4. _____
   Proverbs 10:19, 17:9, 28

1. _____
   Proverbs 15:14 TLB

2. _____
   Romans 8:5

3. _____
   Proverbs 24:2, 12

4. _____
   Proverbs 17:4

DISCOVERY 5: REMAINING COMMITTED TO A GOOD REPORT

Congratulations! You've decided to pull with a winning team. (You have, haven't you?) God will give you the strength to persevere as you tug on his side. Look up each of the following references and complete the list of specific things that encourage consistency in giving good reports.

1. Phil. 4:8 _____

_____

2. Eph. 4:3 _____

3. Prov. 17:9 _____

4. Eph. 4:29 _____

5. Jer. 15:19 _____

6. Prov. 15:28 _____

7. a. Prov. 16:23 _____

   b. How? James 1:5, 1:19; Matt. 12:34; Ps. 37:30 _____

8. Ps. 17:3 _____

DISCOVERY 6: APPLICATION

1. Answer the following questions on your personal tongue habits. Circle the answers that best describe you.

   a. I give good reports:

      1) Always

      2) Sometimes

      3) Seldom

      4) Never

   b. I used my tongue in a good way this week by:

      1) Giving advice to a friend who asked for help

      2) Singing

      3) Encouraging someone

      4) Witnessing of Jesus

      5) Comforting someone

      6) Teaching someone

      7) Expressing love

      8) Asking for needed help for myself or others

      9) Exhorting someone in love

10) Defending a person or a cause that God would defend

11) Expressing concern

12) Praising someone

2. a. Sometimes we lose in this tugging contest. Read the following list of bad uses of the tongue. Using the letters A, B, and C, note which three options *you* abuse most. (Use A for your biggest offense, B for the second biggest, etc.) Then, with the numbers 1, 2, and 3, note which qualities offend you most in other people. (Use 1 for that which bothers you most, 2 for the second most, etc.)

____ Grumble	____ Flatter
____ Slander	____ Gossip
____ Argue	____ Boast
____ Talk too much	____ Being foolish
____ Jest coarsely	____ Lie and exaggerate
____ Curse	____ Being ungrateful

b. What will you do about the results you discovered? __
_____

3. How can you refuse to pay attention to a malicious tongue as mentioned in Prov. 17:4? Are you willing? _____
_____
_____

4. How can you "utter worthy, not worthless, words" as mentioned in Jer. 15:19? Will you? _____
_____
_____

A Parting Thought

"Sometimes my mind is on rewind and my mouth is on fast forward."[1]

---

[1] Dialogue spoken by the character, Arnold, on the television sitcom "Different Strokes."

8

HELPING HANDS
Being a Life-Sharer

Memory Verse: Gal. 6:2

My heart sank to my feet, but I mustered enough energy to bark silently at God. "How could you allow this to happen, Lord?" The costumed children were forming a circle inside the larger wreath of parents ready with generous supplies of Halloween candy. It was the church's "Sweet Spirit" party— our alternative to neighborhood trick or treating. The family games had ended, we'd all admired the costumes based on Scripture verses, and it was time to share treats. "O God, this is a delight for everyone—except a diabetic child." The music started and the children began "the candy march" with their little hands holding sacks that swallowed up the goodies moms had prepared. I whined to my husband, "John, we've got to get him out of here. He isn't going to be able to stay away from all of that sugar."

"No," he replied, "I think we need to let him handle this."

The accompaniment continued. Our insulin-dependent

son stopped at the first adult. She placed a book in his bag. The dad next in line gave him a pencil with his name on it. The third gift was a nicely wrapped package of sugar-free candy. The next stop yielded a bag of pennies, and so on around the circle. God showed his faithfulness to us once again that day. He remembered our son and his unique problem through the love of Christian friends who laid down their lives by sharing our burden.

Getting involved in other people's circumstances is not an option for Christians. We need to share, listen, grieve, intercede, laugh, be available, and love enough to see God's purposes accomplished in another life. It will mean putting ourselves aside. Do you care enough about someone else's life to give them yours?

DISCOVERY 1: LEARNING FROM JONATHAN

Read 1 Sam. 18, 19, and 20, and then read the following account.

The animal skin bag attached to my belt still feels heavy. Four of the five stones are still there because God did the job with one well-aimed missile. I was calm during the battle with Goliath but now it's over and my sweaty legs are exhausted. They feel like they could hold my body up about as well as two of my young lambs could draw Saul's chariot. Men are running in every direction, and in the distance I hear the Philistine shouts of terror mingled with the clear Israeli victory choruses. The sons of Israel are chasing the defeated enemy.

Preparing to face King Saul, I pick up the giant Philistine's head. My lack of fear and abundance of energy to fight the large pagan boggle my mind as I search for the right words to answer the king's questions. It will be difficult to keep my mind trained on the appropriate responses because I'm excited and awestruck. The king of the land will be listening to me—a no-account sheep tender. He'll be hearing my explanation of how God used my efforts.

That scenario is an account of what David might have been feeling as he went to see King Saul after God's victory over the Philistines. David's audience with the king would be like being applauded by the president of the United States for an unexpected act of heroism. However, probably what David longed for most at that moment was a tall, refreshing drink and a close friend to give him an affirming hug and an ear for all the details.

1. a. According to 1 Sam. 18:1, whom did God provide?

_____

b. Who was Jonathan? _____

_____

c. Who was the logical successor to King Saul's throne?

_____

_____

2. It has been said that knowing someone is the sum of shared experiences with that person. Let's look at some of the joint adventures of Jonathan and David. Look up the recommended references on the following chart. Notice Jonathan's response toward David in each circumstance.

Life Situation	Positive or Negative Time for David?	Jonathan's Response
1 Sam 18:1–2, 5		18:1 _____ 18:3 _____ 18:4 _____

Life Situation	Positive or Negative Time for David?	Jonathan's Response
1 Sam. 18:8–9, 12, 15, 16		19:1–2 _____
		19:4–5 _____
1 Sam. 19:1		19:7 _____
1 Sam. 19:9–10, 18, 20		20:1 _____
		20:4 _____
1 Sam. 20:3		20:9 _____
		20:12 _____
		20:16 _____
		20:17 _____
		20:23 _____
1 Sam. 20:24–27		20:28 _____
1 Sam. 20:30–33		20:32 _____
		20:34 _____
1 Sam. 20:35–38		20:39 _____
		20:41 _____
		20:42 _____

3. a. Jonathan stuck by David in all the positive and negative times. Reread the following verses and write down what you think are the keys to this special relationship. 1 Sam. 20:12, 17, 42 _____

b. How did Jonathan live the command Jesus gave in John 15:12–13? _____

DISCOVERY 2: PRACTICALLY SHARING THE BURDENS OF OTHERS

1. Review the following verses and decide how God would have *you* respond in situations calling for life-sharing.

   a. Gal. 6:1–3; 1 Cor. 10:6–12; Lam. 3:39–41a _____

_____

_____

   b. Why should we never be "shocked" by someone else's sin? _____

_____

   c. How do Rom. 14:1 and 15:1–2 help guide you in life-sharing? _____

_____

2. Read 1 Thess. 5:14. What directions does Paul give us for the four groups of people mentioned?

Direction		*People*
a. _____	the	_____
b. _____	the	_____
c. _____	the	_____
d. _____	the	_____

3. Read 1 Cor. 16:17–18.

   a. Paul was excited about the arrival of three friends. In v. 18, what does he say these life-sharers did? _____

_____

b. According to v. 17, how did they manage to be a refreshment? _____

_____

4. Read Deut. 5:5 and Ezek. 22:30.

a. What place is God asking you to take on behalf of your friend? _____

_____

b. According to James 5:16, what is one way to do that?

_____

5. a. What can you offer someone needing help, according to Prov. 15:23? _____

_____

b. To whom should you look to supply those words (Exod. 4:10–12)? _____

c. Why are "pat" answers often not helpful? _____

_____

d. What is the warning shared in 1 Cor. 4:20? _____

_____

e. Under what three circumstances should we share words (Eph. 4:29; see also Col. 4:6)?

1) _____

2) _____

3) _____

6. a. Sometimes we're called *not* to speak. Record what Prov. 17:27–28 says. _____

_____

b. If we're not talking, what does it make sense that we should do? _____

c. God hears the emotion behind our words. In what way does Ps. 116:1–2 illustrate this? _____

_____

d. What can you motivate your burdened friend to do according to Ps. 46:10, 40:1; Isa. 40:28–31? _____

_____

7. a. When someone comes to you with a burden, what does Prov. 25:20 warn you about? _____

_____

b. Has this ever happened to you? _____

c. How did it affect you? _____

_____

d. How do you think it affected the other person? _____

_____

8. Read 1 John 3:16–18.

a. What do these verses counsel us to do? _____

_____

b. How can you "open your heart" to another person? __

_____

c. According to Luke 21:1–4, is the amount of the gift what's important? _____

_____

d. What *is* important? _____

_____

Keep in mind that the best life-sharers are:

1) humble

2) accepting and uncritical

3) a refreshment (supplying what's lacking)

4) prayer warriors

5) able to give timely words

6) good listeners

7) not boasters of their own good news

8) givers

DISCOVERY 3: THE RESULTS OF LIFE-SHARING

Look up the verses on the helping hand below to see what happens when you stoop down to pick someone else up.

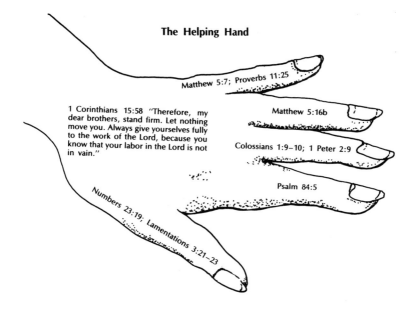

The Helping Hand

Matthew 5:7; Proverbs 11:25

1 Corinthians 15:58 "Therefore, my dear brothers, stand firm. Let nothing move you. Always give yourselves fully to the work of the Lord, because you know that your labor in the Lord is not in vain."

Matthew 5:16b

Colossians 1:9–10; 1 Peter 2:9

Psalm 84:5

Numbers 23:19; Lamentations 3:21–23

DISCOVERY 4: IF NO ONE SHARES MY LIFE

1. Who is the source of our provision according to Rom. 8:32 and Phil. 4:19? _____

_____

_____

_____

2. John 14 paints a picture of Jesus as the Ultimate Encourager. We are told repeatedly that he has a plan, he cares, he's in control, he is "enough." What command is given in John 14:31 following the discourse that begs "do not let your hearts be troubled"? _____

_____

_____

_____

3. After the wall was rebuilt, Nehemiah remembered God's great deeds for his people in the wilderness. In Neh. 9:15, he says "You told them to go in and take possession of the land you had sworn with uplifted hand to give them." What do you think he meant? _____

_____

_____

_____

So—if no one shares your burden, tell Jesus your hurt. Get up and share someone else's burden.

DISCOVERY 5: APPLICATION

Rate yourself on the "Burden-Bearer Chart" that follows. Resolve to strengthen your weak areas and maintain your strong points.

Burden-bearer	Always	Almost Always	Frequently	Sometimes	Never
1. I ask God to help me see the needs of others.					
2. I am willing to be a life-sharer.					
3. I identify with another's problems.					
4. I maintain a positive attitude.					
5. I am willing to persevere in helping another, even if it's hurtful for me and my position.					
6. I recognize my own capability to sin.					
7. I am gentle.					
8. I do not reject help when I need it.					
9. My motive in helping others is to glorify God.					
10. I have God's interests at heart.					
11. I am committed to my friends.					
12. I give sacrificially.					
13. I am a protector.					
14. I am committed to a good report.					

Burden-bearer	Always	Almost Always	Frequently	Sometimes	Never
15. I am a reconciler.					
16. I am a trustworthy confidant.					
17. I consult God as I help others.					
18. I'm not afraid to share my emotions with the friend whose life I share.					
19. I release my friends to be dependent on God.					
20. I allow and encourage others to be all they can be in God's plan.					
21. I purpose to recognize people by the spirit not the flesh.					
22. I refresh others by supplying what is lacking.					
23. I am a faithful intercessor.					
24. I rely on God to direct my words.					
25. I'm a good listener.					
26. I don't tell my good news to a troubled heart.					

1. What concerns of others do you need to give attention to today? _____

_____

_____

2. What friend(s) are you sharing your life with right now?

_____

3. With whom would you like to be a life-sharer? _____

_____

Pray about question 3, asking God for his input.

A Parting Thought

"A Christian is a mind through which Christ thinks,
a heart through which Christ loves,
a voice through which Christ speaks,
a hand through which Christ helps."[1]

—*Guideposts*

---

[1] Lloyd Cory, ed., *Quotable Quotations* (Wheaton, Illinois: Victor Books, a division of Scripture Press Publications, Inc., 1985), 65.

9

CHOOSING SECOND PLACE
Being a Builder of Success in Others

Memory Verse: Phil. 2:3–4

There were only a few weeks left before the end of the year for the fifth grade Sunday school class. "The prizes are great this quarter," April thought, as she anticipated her fourth win for the year. "Last time no one even came near how many Bible verses I memorized, and I remembered to bring my Bible every Sunday. If it weren't for my pokey brothers I wouldn't have any late marks on the attendance sheet." She breezed into Sunday school with a confident air and felt good about herself. As the days wore on, however, April began to think she was feeling a little "too good" about herself. One idea kept pestering her.

"Anyone with half a mind and a little stubbornness could win the Sunday school award," she conceded. "Maybe this time I should prod somebody else to be the winner. Naw. That's dumb. Besides, I really want those treats myself, and no one has ever won four times in a row. It would be a first."

She ran out to play but couldn't keep up the phony carefree attitude. The familiar thoughts kept returning like bothersome flies and April mentally swatted at them. After several miserable days of the "tug-of-war" in her mind, the eleven-year-old decided to encourage her friend Johnny to beat the champion. "Am I nuts? I'm trying to get him to finish ahead of me." And did she try! Johnny won the fourth quarter award and April marked the occasion with a homemade cake for the victor.

She taught herself, one pleased boy, and many astonished adults that we can lay down our lives by choosing to help someone else come in first—even ahead of ourselves.

DISCOVERY 1: WHAT IS SUCCESS?

1. Read each Scripture reference in the following chart and record how and why each person was successful.

Reference	Person	How Successful?	Why Successful?
Gen. 39:2–4, 20–23	Joseph		
1 Sam. 3:19	Samuel		
1 Sam. 16:18, 17:37, 45	David		
2 Kings 18:7 2 Chron. 31:20–21	King Hezekiah		

2. a. Read Phil. 3:4–6. What success did Saul enjoy? _____

Before Saul's conversion he was a great success in the world's eyes, but a loser from the viewpoint of the early

Christians. He had a great zeal, but it was misdirected. He was highly educated, but had misdirected knowledge of the real God. He had a prestigious heritage, being a Hebrew of Hebrews from the tribe of Benjamin, but he wasn't a part of God's true family of believers. As a Pharisee he kept the letter of the law, but he didn't serve the Lord. Although a proud Roman citizen, he was an alien in God's kingdom. He was circumcised on the eighth day, but had an untouched heart. He was blameless by his own standards, but not as God would measure.

Then, according to Acts 9, on the road to Damascus Saul became Paul.

b. What is Paul's definition of success in Phil. 3:7–14?

_____

c. What truths can you apply to your life from Phil. 4:13 and John 15:5? _____

_____

d. What is the psalmist's testimony in Ps. 73:28? _____

_____

e. What is your honest opinion right now? _____

_____

3. Read Josh. 1:7–8. The Hebrew definition of success is "to act wisely." What one word tells how we can act wisely? (See the following references for help: Josh. 1:7–8; Deut. 28:1–12, 29:9; 1 Chron. 22:13; Prov. 13:21; Matt. 7:24–27.) _____

_____

_____

4. a. Using the verses below, cite ways to learn obedience.

1) Ps. 1:1–3; Josh. 1:8 _____

2) Ps. 27:8; 2 Chron. 26:5 _____

3) Ps. 25:12–13; Prov. 28:26 _____

4) Heb. 5:8 _____

b. How do you delight in God's Word? _____

_____

c. How have you sought his face today? _____

_____

d. In what areas are you not trusting God? _____

_____

e. How has suffering made you more obedient? _____

_____

5. If you accept the premise that God is the source of real success and that acting wisely is ultimate prosperity, then what is the logical way to help someone else become successful? (For help see 2 Cor. 2:14–15, 5:14–21; 1 Peter 3:15; 2 Peter 1:1–5; Col. 1:28; Phil. 1:20–25; Col. 2:6–7.) _

_____

_____

6. Why does God delight in the success of his people, according to Ps. 35:27? _____

_____

DISCOVERY 2: LEARNING FROM DEBORAH

Read Judges 4.

Do you remember the old game show "Truth or Consequences"? The book of Judges is like that TV program. When

Israel walked in God's truth, they received blessing. When they walked away from God's truth, the consequences were negative. The judges were sent as God's act of mercy to help a wayward people out of their messes. Deborah was one of those judges. Let's consider this remarkable woman and some of the traits that helped her make Barak successful.

1. What does God tell us about Deborah in Judg. 4:4? ____

_____

2. According to vv. 2 and 7, what can we learn about Sisera? _____

_____

3. Why was Jabin's army a threat to the Israelites (see v. 2)? _____

_____

4. How does v. 1 explain why God would sell Israel into the hands of Jabin? _____

_____

5. a. According to v. 6, who was sought out by Deborah to lead the defense against this powerful army? _____

b. By whose command did Deborah make this request of Barak? _____

c. How does that indicate that Deborah was "in tune" with God? _____

_____

6. a. What is the promise of v. 7? _____

_____

b. What was Barak's response in v. 8? _____

_____

c. What does that reveal about his character? _____

_____

7. a. What did Deborah do, according to vv. 9 and 10? ___

_____

b. How did she exhibit faithfulness to her promises and to God? _____

_____

c. How did she direct Barak to depend on and thus honor God? _____

_____

8. From your experience, what is the value of working side by side with someone under God's authority? _____

_____

9. What techniques did Deborah use to motivate Barak in v. 14? _____

_____

10. How does v. 15 reveal that Deborah was a good discerner of God's timing? _____

_____

11. a. What in v. 16 reveals that Barak was a "finisher"?

_____

b. How does this verse indicate that Deborah allowed Barak to be God's instrument in this circumstance? _____

_____

12. How do you think Deborah worked to help *complete* Barak rather than *compete* with him? _____

_____

13. Read vv. 17–24. What impresses you about the rest of the story? _____

_____

_____

14. a. Read Chapter 5. According to this chapter, what did Deborah lead Barak to do? _____

b. What was the first thing Deborah praised God for in v. 2? _____

_____

c. How would this have encouraged Barak? _____

_____

15. What positive consequence to Deborah's actions is recorded in the last sentence of 5:31? _____

_____

16. What have you learned from Deborah's example? ____

_____

_____

17. Right now ask God to give you the name of one person you should be helping to make successful. *Whom* do you have in mind to build up? _____

DISCOVERY 3: BUILDING UP SOMEONE ELSE

In Discovery 2 you decided whom you might work at making successful, following Deborah's pattern. Consider making a commitment to the Lord in the declaration to follow. Remember, God takes vows very seriously, so if you're not ready to make the commitment now, please don't. (See Eccl. 5:4–5.)

Look at the following references and determine how you can practically follow Deborah's example. Write these practical applications on the chart that follows.

Deborah's Example	How We Could Do It
Tuned in to God	Luke 22:31–32; Josh. 1:8; Jer. 33:3; Ps. 27:8
Willing	Phil. 2:13; Col. 1:9–12; Isa. 6:8; Ezek. 22:30
Faithful	Luke 16:10; Matt. 11:28–30

Deborah's Example	How We Could Do It
Glorifying God	John 16:13−14; Eph. 5:18; John 17:4; 6:29
Discerning	Heb. 5:12−6:1a
A Completor	Col. 1:28; John 12:32; 1 Cor. 2:2; 2 Cor. 5:14−16
Worshipful	Heb. 13:15−18; 1 Chron. 16:4; John 12:32; 2 Chron. 7:3

declaration of commitment

I will, with god's help:

listen for god's directions

be willing to act on those directions

be faithful to my promises

give god the credit for victory

work with my friend under
    god's authority

discern the best procedure and timing

be a completor, not a competitor

lead the other person into praise
    of god for the success achieved

signed: _____

this _____ day of _____, 19___.

    witness: _____

DISCOVERY 4: DRAWING ATTENTION AWAY FROM MYSELF

Look up the following verses and, after each reference, record your thoughts on drawing attention away from yourself.

1. John 3:30 _____

2. 2 Cor. 5:14–15 _____

3. 1 Tim. 6:6 _____

4. 1 John 3:16 _____

5. 1 Cor. 1:31; Jer. 9:23 _____

6. James 4:10 _____

7. Mark 10:45 _____

8. On the blanks provided below, rewrite Phil. 2:3–4 in your own words. _____

_____

_____

_____

DISCOVERY 5: APPLICATION

In this lesson you may have decided to make an important commitment to help a specific person succeed.

1. How are you listening intently for God's direction? _____

_____

2. How will you act on those directions? _____

_____

3. How are you planning to be faithful to your promises? __

_____

4. How will you work side by side with your friend, under God's authority? _____

_____

5. How can you give the credit to God for the victory? _____

_____

6. What are the procedures and timing you can discern in this situation? _____

_____

7. a. How will you help to complete this person? _____

_____

b. In what ways could you shy away from competitiveness? _____

8. What time have you set aside to praise God in this situation? _____

A Parting Thought

"A self-centered life is totally empty,
while an emptied life allows room for God."
—*Tom Haggai*[1]

---

[1] Lloyd Cory, ed., *Quotable Quotations* (Wheaton, Illinois: Victor Books, a division of Scripture Press Publications, Inc., 1985), 344.

10

LOOKING IN THE KEYHOLE
Being Cheerfully Hospitable

Memory Verse: 1 Peter 4:9

The guttural voice didn't seem to match the dancing eyes and broad smile. "I'm Valter and I'm here!" It sounded more like he was clearing his German throat than greeting his American hosts.

Walter had indeed "arrived." It was late in the evening and the house was a mess because we had been absorbed in a sixth grade film-making project. There were props, film clips, and snacks strewn everywhere. I was weary. The children were in that scary stage of "beyond tired and threatening to get a second wind." And, Walter was at the door.

We were his first of many stops across the United States after he arrived at Kennedy International Airport. Our contact in Germany had told us he *might* come, but his expected date of arrival had long passed. He was to stay with Americans across the land to become acquainted with the home of the free and the brave. *I* felt anything but free or brave. I was enslaved to three weary kids, there were dustballs under the bed, and I wanted to cower behind my husband and have him deliver the bad news to Walter: "Sorry pal, we don't know what you're talking about. No room here." Slam!

However, we pulled ourselves together, readied the bedroom for our unexpected stranger, filled his stomach, and listened to his tales of finding our remote farm lane in a town not even marked on a recent map. The two weeks he stayed with us began what has turned into a friendship spanning the seas and the years. He is, without a doubt, the most unforgettable character in our lives, and banging the door in Walter's face that October night would have robbed us of a sweet chapter in our lives.

Most believers can be persuaded to open their homes in hospitality. But when we do it cheerfully we have a chance to lay down our lives. Let's learn how to not rob ourselves of the guests God brings our way.

DISCOVERY 1: BEING HOSPITABLE

Look up each of the following verses and on the following "Key to my Heart and Home" illustration record to whom God says we should offer hospitality.

1 Peter 4:9	Heb. 12:12–13
1 Tim. 5:8	Luke 14:13–14
Heb. 13:2	Rom. 12:20
Matt. 25:35	Isa. 35:3–4

Key to My Heart and Home

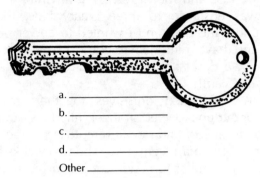

a. _____

b. _____

c. _____

d. _____

Other _____

DISCOVERY 2: LEARNING FROM THE SHUNAMMITE WOMAN

Read 2 Kings 4:8–17, and we'll study it verse by verse.

V. 8
Key No. 1
Sensitivity

How was the Shunammite woman alert to the needs of people?

_____

V. 8
Key No. 2
Availability

What do the words *whenever he came by* indicate about the availability of the woman?

_____

V. 8
Key No. 3
Flexibility

The verse tells us that the woman was "well-to-do." How does this imply that she would have had many other things to do besides look out her window for people to help?

_____

V. 8
Key No. 4

How does this verse say she got Elisha to eat her food? _____

Persuasiveness   How can urging, or being persuasive, work to make others feel welcome in your home? _____

V. 9
Key No. 5   What did the woman realize about
Perceptivity   Elisha? _____
(Discernment)   How would knowing that Elisha was a man of God change her treatment of him if she, too, was a follower of Jehovah? _____
How would the treatment differ if she had her back turned on God? _____

VV. 9–10
Key No. 6   Whom did the woman talk to about
Submissiveness Elisha? _____
How does this indicate that she desired to remain under authority in the opening of their home? _____
How is it clear that her husband was her priority? _____

V. 10
Key No. 7   How does this verse indicate that the
Generosity   woman met needs with the resources available?

_____

V. 10
Key No. 8   A room was added to the Shunam-
Preparedness   mite's house to accommodate visitors. How does this action indicate the woman's desire to be prepared? _____
How do you think she could have prepared spiritually for her role as a hostess? _____

V. 13
Key No. 9
Carefulness
(diligence)

Elisha said that the woman had "gone to all this trouble for us." The NASB translates this as "careful." How was she "careful" for them?

_____

VV. 13–17
Key No. 10
Receptivity

Elisha's logical question, after so much generosity, was "what can be done for you?"
Describe the woman's response. _____

_____

DISCOVERY 3: A PROPER ATMOSPHERE FOR GUESTS

Look at each reference on the following chart and on the blanks jot down the important ideas.

References	I Can Offer an Atmosphere of:
1. Prov. 15:17	_____
2. 1 Cor. 16:19; Acts 18:23–26	_____
3. 1 Thess. 2:8	_____
4. Titus 1:8–9	_____
5. Titus 2:7–8	_____
6. Rom. 12:10–12	_____
7. Rom. 12:18	_____

DISCOVERY 4: THE DANGERS IN HOSPITALITY

Read the following verses and fill in the chart below to recognize potential problems.

Reference	God's Exhortation	Hospitality Problem to Avoid
1. Eph. 4:29		
2. Prov. 23:2		
3. Matt. 6:33 Acts 17:11 1 Thess. 5:17		
4. Gal. 1:10		

DISCOVERY 5: THE RESPONSIBILITIES OF ONE *RECEIVING* HOSPITALITY

Let's turn the tables. So far, we've been seeking God's mind on loving the folks who stay in our homes. We have learned to be servants, laying down our lives, in cheerful hospitality. What attitudes should be ours when we are guests in someone else's home?

Read Luke 9:6. The disciples were going out from village to village.

1. What two verbs describe what they did as they stayed in each place?

a. _____

b. _____

The Greek definitions of the words in this verse are significant. *Preaching* comes from the Greek word *euaggelizo* that means "to announce glad tidings."[1] *Healing* is translated from the Greek word *therapeuo,* that means "to serve or cure."[2] Our word *therapeutic* is derived from it.

2. Think about the last time you were a guest in someone's home. How specifically could you have acted to "announce glad tidings"? _____

_____

3. a. Would a joyful or crabby attitude be most helpful in following God's ways? _____

b. Why? _____

4. How specifically could you have been a therapeutic influence—serving and healing? _____

_____

5. What will you do next time you visit someone's home?

_____

There you have it! We need to offer hospitality as servants. And, we need to *receive* hospitality as servants.

[1] *New American Standard Exhaustive Concordance of the Bible,* 1652.
[2] Ibid., 1655.

DISCOVERY 6: APPLICATION

1. Is it sometimes easier to be hospitable to strangers than to our own families? Why? _____

_____

2. a. How hospitable are you to your immediate family? Following is a list of things you might consider doing for guests visiting your home. Place a check next to the items in that list that you have done for your spouse and children in the last week.

1) Awakened early to prepare breakfast _____

2) Made sack lunches for people leaving home that day _____

3) Made a special dessert _____

4) Prepared a special snack, ready to eat when children arrived home _____

5) Arranged to be home when they arrived _____

b. What other ideas do you have for being as hospitable to your family as to guests in your home? _____

_____

3. a. Why is it important to be "under authority" and considerate to your family while offering hospitality to others? _____

_____

b. What effects might there be if you did what your spouse or roommate *wouldn't* want you to do? _____

_____

4. a. How is it true that if your heart is open to God and people, your home will be too? _____

_____

    b. What practical things could you do to show openness and consideration in your home? _____

_____

5. a. Consider the last time you had guests in your home. Rate yourself on the chart to follow. Check the appropriate columns and see where your strengths and weaknesses are.

I Was	Yes	Some-what	No
Sensitive			
Available			
Flexible			
Persuasive			
Perceptive			
Submissive			
Generous			
Priority-Conscious			
Careful			
Prepared			
Diligent			
Receptive			
The Atmosphere of My Home Provided and Motivated:	**Yes**	**Some-what**	**No**
Love			
Growth			
Sincerity			
Caring			

The Atmosphere of My Home Provided and Motivated:	Yes	Some-what	No
Steadfastness Examples of Good Deeds Prayerfulness Giving Preference to Others Peace			

b. How could you have improved? _____

_____

c. What strengths will you try to maintain next time you have a chance to be hospitable? _____

_____

6. a. What dangers in hospitality have you experienced?

Gluttony? _____

Idle talk? _____

Inattention to God and his Word? _____

Trying to impress people? _____

b. Share a specific situation. _____

c. What can you do to remedy the problem area? _____

_____

A Parting Thought

We would be wise to treat
our family as guests
and our guests as family.

11

KEYBOARD HARMONY
Being a Lover of the Unlovely

Memory Verse: Matt. 5:46—48

"I wish I had a dime for every time she says 'me' in her endless monologues," I sneered. "She's a master manipulator and she holds the self-bestowed honor of 'authority on every subject.' To make matters worse, she has the nerve to be impatient with anyone who disagrees with her." Teeth clenched, I winced at my now familiar reaction to this woman.

Even more amazing than how obnoxious the woman is, is the love my friend, Carol Plum, offers each time she is in the company of this woman. "I know Carol has a knack with people, but even she can't possibly see anything positive in the lady's immaturity," I thought, trying to excuse my own bad attitude. Wishing I could be like Carol, I mused: "What is her secret?"

Simply stated, the secret is in laying down our lives by loving the unlovely. We can choose to create a beautiful symphony, even with the relationships that throw us most out of tune.

Good piano playing offers beautiful melodies. Even the dissonance of black and white keys played together contribute to harmony if the base note provides a strong foundation for the chord. If all notes had the same sound and were played in exactly the same way, there would be no harmony. We'd hear a boring monotone; hardly a delight to even the most untrained ear.

Our lives *can* be harmonious if the foundation for our relationships is grounded in Jesus Christ. Then, people completely different from us—and even disagreeable to us— can provide beautiful orchestration. The Master's hand can tune potential dissonance in people so that they contribute to a pleasing melody. For this to happen, however, we must be willing to learn to love those unlovely to us.

DISCOVERY 1: THE IMPORTANCE OF LOVING ALL PEOPLE

Look up the following references and answer the questions.

1. Rom. 14:19–20. Whose work is torn down when you do not work toward mutual edification? _____

2. a. Job 23:13–14. According to v. 13, is anyone like God? _____

b. What in v. 14 makes you think he has a specific plan for each individual? _____

---

c. When you choose not to love others, what are you saying about the uniqueness God gives to each person? _____

---

124 ● A Workshop on Self-Giving

3. a. John 13:34–35. What does God ask you to do? _____

_____

b. Why should you follow his example? _____

_____

c. Are these verses a command or a suggestion? _____

d. What is a disciple's proper response to any of God's commands? _____

_____

4. a. 2 Cor. 5:14–17. What compels believers? _____

_____

b. How did Christ exhibit this special love? _____

_____

c. Whom should we be living for? _____

_____

d. Find the word "so" in v. 16. On the basis of all the preceding facts mentioned in vv. 14–17, what can we now do? _____

_____

e. V. 17 says that everyone, once they meet and submit themselves to Christ is a "new creation." We don't have to recognize anyone according to the flesh. The unlovely things about people don't have to push us away from them. That means we can love ourselves, our spouses, our children, our roommates, our friends, our friends' children, our parents, etc. How does loving yourself free you to love others? _____

_____

5. a. Read 2 Cor. 10:12. What is the problem mentioned here? _____

_____

b. What kind of people compare themselves with themselves, according to this verse? _____

_____

c. How does James 2:4 add to the meaning of this principle? _____

_____

6. 1 Sam. 16:7. What do we neglect when we reject someone because of an obvious problem? _____

_____

7. a. 1 John 4:20. When we withhold love from someone, whom are we rejecting? _____

_____

b. According to this verse, how is the unloving person described? _____

_____

DISCOVERY 2: WHY CERTAIN ONES ARE UNLOVELY

1. Look at Isa. 53:2–4, 7. What characteristics made this person unlovely? _____

_____

_____

2. a. Look at Isa. 53:11 for more clues. Whom is this describing? _____

b. According to Rev. 4:11 and Rom. 4:8, is he worth our love? _____

c. Why? _____

_____

3. Read Rom. 1:21–32. What one word could label all the unlovely people described in this passage? _____

_____

4. a. Read Rom. 3:10–18, 23. How many people are guilty of this problem? _____

_____

b. According to these verses, are *you* guilty? _____

5. Read Rom. 5:6–8. What do we see is God's response to these unlovely ones? _____

_____

6. Study the list of qualities following. Choose eight that represent things that make others most unlovely to you. Place those eight characteristics on the white piano keys in the octave on the full-page illustration that follows Discovery 3. Now choose six qualities that you think might make you most offensive to others. Place those on the black keys. Look at your personalized octave and see how you think it would be possible to get in tune with others as you allow Jesus to be the note that resolves the chord.

dishonest	elderly	poor
untruthful	discourteous	lazy
boastful	forgetful	insincere
divorced	silly	violent
compulsive	know-it-all	alcoholic
tardy	narrowminded	cruel
skinny	handicapped	unhygienic
timid	unreliable	nosy
aloof	wealthy	drug-addicted

snobbish	inarticulate	disloyal
bossy	unforgiving	pessimistic
non-American	hostile	talkative
gambler	conceited	irresponsible
impatient	foul-mouthed	nonathletic
bad-tempered	disrespectful	foolish
racist	insensitive	pretentious
criminal	loud	unskilled
careless	moody	rude
impudent	undisciplined	unattentive
disrespectful	religious	gossipy
whiny	stubborn	arrogant
mischievous	dull	mentally ill
obese	self-righteous	unattractive
sexually immoral	money-hungry	ungrateful
ill-mannered	selfish	optimistic
selfish	politically extreme	superstitious
overdisciplined	unapologetic	

—Others not on the list?—

(If you're in a Bible study group, you may want to choose eleven people to put their octaves side by side. Then observe what the whole keyboard looks like and how harmony could be possible.)

DISCOVERY 3: PAUL WAS UNLOVELY TO ANANIAS

The Ananias of this study is not the Ananias of Acts 5. Paul and Saul are the same man. His name was Saul before meeting Christ, and was changed to Paul after his conversion.

1. Read Paul's defense to King Agrippa in Acts 26:9–11. Suppose you were a Christian jury member at a trial for Saul. How would you feel about him? _____

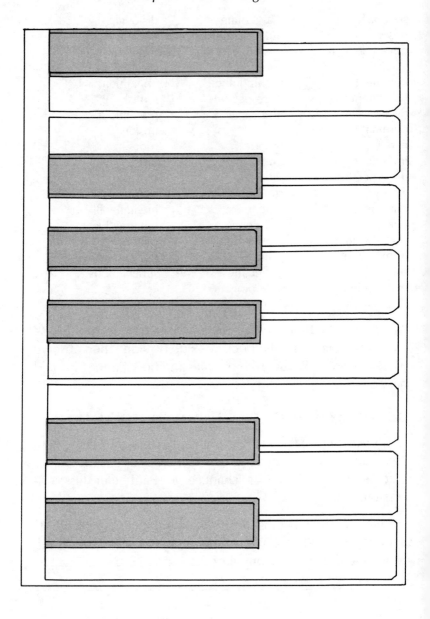

2. Read Phil. 3:4–6. Why did Paul have reason to be arrogant and boastful? List his credentials. _____

_____

_____

3. a. Read Acts 9:10. How is Ananias described? _____

_____

_____

b. Why do you think the Lord chose Ananias to help Saul? _____

_____

c. Do you think Ananias was proud or humble? Why? __

_____

d. Why or why not are Paul and Ananias likely candidates for a close relationship? _____

_____

DISCOVERY 4: LEARNING FROM ANANIAS'S LOVE OF PAUL

Read the dramatic story of Paul's conversion in Acts 9:1–31.

1. Reread vv. 6, 10–12. How did God prepare the hearts of Saul and Ananias to receive each other? _____

_____

2. a. Read vv. 13–14. What was Ananias's response to God? _____

_____

b. What was Ananias's opinion of Saul based on? _____

_____

c. What details did Ananias share with God? _____

_____

3. a. Reread vv. 15–16. What was God's one-word challenge to Ananias? _____

b. What do you think was God's reasoning behind his command? _____

_____

4. a. Refer to v. 17a. What indicates that Ananias obeyed God? _____

_____

b. What expectations did Ananias have to relinquish in order to obey? _____

_____

5. a. Look at v. 17b. With what words did Ananias greet Saul? _____

_____

b. How did his greeting indicate a desire to find a common ground? _____

_____

c. How do you think this indicated that Ananias visualized success in the relationship? _____

_____

6. Reread v. 17c. Why, specifically, did God send Ananias to Saul? _____

_____

7. According to vv. 18–22, 28, what good came to Paul as a result of Ananias's efforts? _____

_____

_____

8. Reread v. 25. What were the other disciples motivated to do because of Ananias's initial love action? _____

_____

9. Look at v. 31. What results occurred in the church because of Ananias's reluctant, but obedient, love? _____

_____

DISCOVERY 5: APPLICATION

1. Think of one person in your life right now who is hard for you to love. (Write a first name only.) _____

_____

2. Identify why this person is unlovely to you. _____

_____

3. Ask God for his love for that person.

4. How do you think God may be preparing your heart and the other person's heart to receive each other? _____

_____

5. What details about that person have you shared with God? If you haven't shared with God—do it now. _____

_____

6. What expectations will you have to relinquish in order to obey God's command to love that person? _____

_____

7. What common ground can you find with this person? ___

_____

8. What success can you visualize in your relationship? ___

_____

9. What purposes do you think God is attempting to accomplish in your life and the other person's life as a result of your gift of love? _____

_____

A Parting Thought

> *"Love cures people—*
> *both the ones who give it*
> *and the ones who receive it."*
>
> —Karl Menninger

12

WHISTLE WHILE YOU WORK
Being an Excellent Example in the Mundane

Memory Verse: Luke 16:10

The strain wasn't enough to wipe the smile off the woman's middle-aged face. It was the third piece of sound equipment she and her sister had moved. "Only one more concert on this week's schedule," she encouraged the other woman.

The woman's brother-in-law was recovering from surgery, and to meet the bills, her sister continued in the music ministry she shared with her husband. In addition to moving equipment, the woman provided a "second home" for the children, prayed for the medically troubled family, and provided the hugs necessary for the younger sister struggling with the emotions of the situation. It's fun providing stage-crew muscles and smiles, she thought, and it's great having little ones around again.

The results of mundane tasks often are not noticed unless the job is neglected or poorly done. Yet, those jobs well done often carry the greatest rewards. Piano accompanists can make or break a great solo. A diligent cleaning crew can set the stage for a successful business conference. A nurse who provides the right instruments in the correct order makes the surgeon look competent. A smart caddy aids the golfer in an eighteen-hole win.

Ruth is an example of excellence in the mundane. Though low on the Bethlehem social ladder, she was young, poor, a widow—and an alien to boot. To satisfy daily food needs this Moabitess humbled herself by picking up the wheat that others left behind in the fields. It would be like rifling through lines of suburban trash cans today. However, in time, Ruth became the joint-owner of all the fields she gleaned, partly because of her faithfulness in little things. We would do well to imitate Ruth's actions and attitudes.

Have you ever resented doing mundane jobs? Does your attitude honor Christ and encourage others as you toil over a large pile of mending, or clean someone else's bathroom mess, or rinse a mud-stained car after a friend borrowed it—when it was clean? We can learn to be practical in laying down our lives, by doing mundane things with excellence. God's strength and smile will cheer us on as we persevere in the completion of every task as if we were doing it just for him. We can fold Jesus' socks, clean his sink, mow his lawn, type God's dissertation, and pick up his toys with a glad heart. Let's learn how together.

DISCOVERY 1: IT'S HARD TO DO

1. What attitude does our society teach about taking responsibility for doing mundane things well, especially things that no one observes? _____

_____

2. a. What do we learn from Samuel in 1 Sam. 16:7? _____

_____

b. How does Jesus expand on this teaching in his conversation with the Pharisees in Luke 11:37–44? _____

_____

3. a. Read Luke 10:20. What were the disciples excited about? _____

_____

b. What did Jesus say they should be excited about? _____

_____

c. If their names were recorded in the Book of Life, what would that indicate? _____

_____

d. What is the important truth in this passage? _____

_____

4. What further command is given in 1 Cor. 10:31? _____

_____

5. Do you believe that the mother who does an excellent job of washing soiled diapers with a sweet spirit is just as pleasing to the Lord as the internationally known evangelist who leads many thousands into a right relationship with God? _____
Why or why not? _____

_____

DISCOVERY 2: LEARNING FROM RUTH

"If I hear her complain one more time, I think I'll scream," Ruth thought, as her mother-in-law whined again. "I don't think she remembers that I'm a widow, too." Naomi's bitterness was beginning to rub Ruth the wrong way. Yet there was something special about Naomi. "My husband had her nose and her smile. Oh, to see his smile again," Ruth thought. Naomi moaned about God's harsh treatment of her and, as a result, Ruth had to take the next step toward the Israelite's homeland with great resolve. "I'd give anything to go back to Moab."

Ruth's fingers carefully sorted her windblown hair as she dismissed that last thought. "I know it's right to follow Naomi and I'll do it for my husband's sake. I want to honor his memory. Besides, Naomi's God keeps inviting me to know more and more about him."

Ruth was a determined young lady. The fictionalized account you've just read gives you an idea of what Ruth's emotions may have been like. Now read Ruth 1:22–2:23 and let's see what attitudes helped her to do commonplace things with excellence.

1. What do you learn about Ruth in 2:7? _____

_____

2. What attitude describes Ruth in 2:10? _____

_____

3. How does 2:12 indicate that God was Ruth's motivating force (also see 1:16)? _____

_____

4. What does 2:23 indicate about Ruth's perseverance? ____

_____

5. According to Ruth 2:21, 3:11, 4:10, 13, 17, what blessings did Ruth receive? _____

_____

DISCOVERY 3: EXCELLENCE IN THE MUNDANE

Look up the exhortations on the following wheat bundle illustration to see what attitudes will help you lay down your life in this way. Record these ten attitudes on a separate piece of paper before going on to Discovery 4.

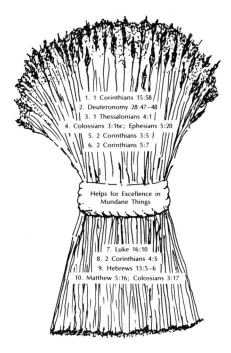

1. 1 Corinthians 15:58
2. Deuteronomy 28:47–48
3. 1 Thessalonians 4:1
4. Colossians 3:16c; Ephesians 5:20
5. 2 Corinthians 3:5
6. 2 Corinthians 5:7

Helps for Excellence in Mundane Things

7. Luke 16:10
8. 2 Corinthians 4:5
9. Hebrews 13:5–6
10. Matthew 5:16; Colossians 3:17

DISCOVERY 4: APPLICATION

1. In what big things have you been faithful to God? _____

_____

2. What mundane jobs are necessary in your life? _____

_____

3. Which of those "little things" do you resent doing most? Why? _____

_____

4. Using the checklist below, try doing those most demeaning jobs "as unto the Lord." Check yourself every time you encounter those tasks and record any changes in your attitudes and actions.

a. I will choose to persevere in this task because it is necessary.

b. I will choose to be joyful in the doing of it.

c. I will choose to be the best worker I can be at this job.

d. I will choose to be grateful for this job, dwelling on the positives, not the negatives. (For example, choosing to be grateful that I own many pieces of clothing, rather than moaning over all the wash that needs to be done.)

e. I choose to recognize that my adequacy for excellence in this job, both in attitude and action, is from God.

f. I choose to believe that God watches and cares how I handle myself in the execution of this work.

g. I choose to be faithful to excellence in this "little thing," knowing it is training me for faithfulness in "big things."

h. I choose to be a servant, even when I'm treated like one.

i. I choose to believe that God works side by side with me as I complete this commonplace task, giving me more time to know him as I do it.

j. I choose to do this job for God's glory and honor, not to impress others.

5. Note changes in your attitudes and actions. _____

A Parting Thought

> "The things that Jesus did
> were of the most menial and commonplace order,
> and this is an indication that it takes
> all God's power in me to do
> the most commonplace things in His way."
> —Oswald Chambers[1]

---

[1] Oswald Chambers, *My Utmost for His Highest* (New York: Dodd, Mead & Co., 1935), 255.

EPILOGUE

Memory Verse: John 13:4—5

> "So he got up from the meal, took off his outer clothing, and wrapped a towel around his waist. After that, he poured water into a basin and began to wash his disciples' feet, drying them with the towel that was wrapped around him."

Even today Jesus is washing our feet. The cleansing comes each time he listens. The cleansing is complete with each forgiveness, as he throws out our sins with the dirty water in the basin. He instructs, he cares, he intercedes, and he strengthens. He accepts the least of our gifts and the best we can offer, and he doesn't care that we sometimes don't even know the difference between our least and our best. He washes us.

His refreshment flows as he lifts up our tired limbs, heals our bones, straightens our paths, encourages our hearts, and smiles at his disciples' purpose for living. We can find comfort, peace, and confidence in his faithful washing, and we can thank him as he motivates us to pursue his likeness.

Get up. Wrap the towel around yourself. Be more watchful of his will. Call for his eyes. Be his hands. Decrease as he increases. Love him more as you lay down your life for others.

The gift goes on. As Jesus says in John 15:12–14:

> "My command is this: Love each other as I have loved you. Greater love has no one than this, that he lay down his life for his friends. You are my friends if you do what I command."